# rocks & minerals

An **EXPLORE YOUR WORLD**™ Handbook

DISCOVERY COMMUNICATIONS
*Founder, Chairman, and Chief Executive Officer:*
John S. Hendricks
*President and Chief Operating Officer:*
Judith A. McHale
*President, Discovery Enterprises Worldwide:*
Michela English

DISCOVERY PUBLISHING
*Vice President, Publishing:* Ann-Marie McGowan
*Publishing Director:* Natalie Chapman
*Editorial Director:* Rita Thievon Mullin
*Senior Editor:* Mary Kalamaras

DISCOVERY CHANNEL RETAIL
*Product Development:* Tracy Fortini
*Naturalist:* Steve Manning

DISCOVERY COMMUNICATIONS, INC., produces high-quality television programming, interactive media, books, films, and consumer products.
DISCOVERY NETWORKS, a division of Discovery Communications, Inc., operates and manages the Discovery Channel, TLC, Animal Planet, and Travel Channel.

*Rocks & Minerals,* An Explore Your World ™ Handbook, was created and produced for DISCOVERY PUBLISHING by ST. REMY MEDIA INC.

**Library of Congress Cataloging-in-Publication Data**
Rocks & minerals: an explore your world handbook.
p. cm.
Includes index.
ISBN 1-56331-803-2
1. Geology. 2. Rocks. 3. Minerals. I. Discovery Channel (Firm) II. Title: Rocks and minerals. III. Title: Rocks & minerals.
QE26.2.D57        1999
552--dc21                        99-14305
                                        CIP

Random House website address:
http://www.atrandom.com
Discovery Channel Online website address:
http://www.discovery.com
Printed in the United States of America on acid-free paper
First Edition   10 9 8 7 6 5 4 3 2 1

CONSULTANTS

**Donald Brobst** had a thirty-year career with the U.S. Geological Survey before turning his interests to education. Author of more than eighty publications, Dr. Brobst is a Senior Fellow of the Mineralogical Society of America. He currently teaches geology at Northern Virginia Community College.

**Anthony R. Kampf** has been Curator of the world-renowned gem and mineral collection at Los Angeles County Museum of Natural History since 1980.

**Joan Kaylor** has been Curator of Mineralogy and Geology for the Redpath Museum at McGill University in Montreal for almost two decades.

**Robert Jones** is Senior Editor of *Rock & Gem* magazine. A graduate of New Haven Teachers College, he has written more than six hundred articles on gems and minerals, and wrote and hosted the television documentary, *Russian Gem Treasures,* later broadcast on PBS. He received the 1998 Carnegie Mineralogical Award.

**George H. McCourt** has Masters degrees in Environmental Science and Geology. He teaches geology at Macdonald College, McGill University.

PHOTOGRAPHER FOR THE IDENTIFICATION GUIDES

**Wendell E. Wilson** is one of the world's foremost mineral photographers and artists, having published more than 6,000 photos and 850 artworks. He is the editor and publisher of *The Mineralogical Record,* which received the 1995 Carnegie Mineralogical Award for outstanding contributions to mineralogy. He is the author of more than three hundred books and journal articles, and is the founder and Director of the Mineralogical Record Library. A new mineral, wendwilsonite, was named for him in 1987.

# rocks &
# minerals

**An EXPLORE
YOUR WORLD™
Handbook**

DISCOVERY BOOKS

NEW YORK

# CONTENTS

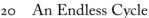

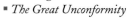

# REALM
# OF ROCKS

# PLANET EARTH

*Earth is composed of rocks and their mineral components,
thus their stories are inextricably linked to the planet's history.*

Rocks and minerals are perhaps so fascinating because they are the very stuff of the world we inhabit. The sheer diversity of their shapes, shades, and textures is staggering. We admire and collect them, haggle over their value, and marvel at their beauty. For scientists the attraction goes far beyond appearance: To understand the origins and composition of rocks and minerals is to understand the birth, evolution, and behavior of the planet.

The story begins about 4.5 billion years ago when Earth was created from celestial debris caught in orbit around a youthful sun. A violent accumulative process produced a mass of dust and rocks composed predominately of a limited number of elements, including iron, silicon, magnesium, oxygen, and aluminum. Meteors, large and small, bombarded the surface. Over time, heat and gravity layered the elements; the denser ones, mostly iron and some nickel, sank toward the center, the lighter elements flowed outward to

**Anatomy of Planet Earth**
*Earth is a multi-layered planet comprised of a core of iron and nickel, a cooler intermediate layer of rock, and a thin cool crust.*

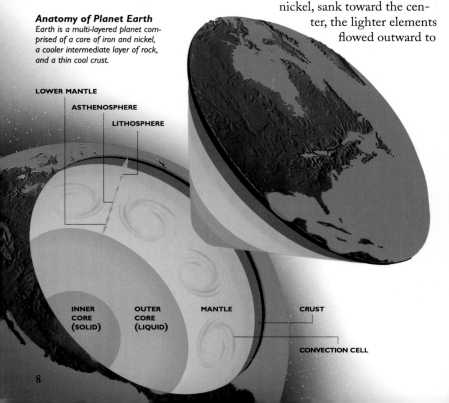

LOWER MANTLE

ASTHENOSPHERE

LITHOSPHERE

INNER CORE (SOLID)

OUTER CORE (LIQUID)

MANTLE

CRUST

CONVECTION CELL

form the planet's uppermost layers, called the mantle and the crust.

The core is now estimated to make up about 16 percent of Earth's mass and the mantle about 83 percent—which leaves only 1 percent for the skinlike crust that we recognize as the land beneath our feet. The Earth's core is unimaginably hot, reaching a temperature of about 13,000°F (7,200°C). The iron should be molten at this temperature—iron melts at about 2,795°F (1,535°C)—but the pressure at the innermost core is so intense that the metal remains solid. Only the outer core, under less pressure, is able to remain in the liquid state.

Unlike the core, the mantle is made of rock, mainly a dark rock called peridotite, which contains iron and magnesium. It is composed of three zones: the immense lower mantle; the warmer, gooey asthenosphere in the middle; and the uppermost mantle, which—along with the overlying crust—constitutes the lithosphere, a region that has excited much scientific attention over the last generation.

### PLATE TECTONICS

Since the 1960s geology has undergone a revolution. Not only has modern technology provided science with many tools for studying the planet—computer modeling, for instance—but geologists also have acquired a unifying theory to help explain how the Earth works. That theory, plate tectonics, proposes that the lithosphere is not a solid shell, but a loose patchwork of a dozen or so large plates and numerous smaller ones that lie below the oceans and the continents.

The plates are created when molten rock, known as magma, oozes up through cracks in the crust called rift zones and crystallizes. The plates that lie beneath the oceans are composed of a variety of igneous (volcanic) rocks. They are thin—about two to five miles (3 to 8 km) thick—but heavy, and ride lower in the mantle. The continental plates are thicker, ranging between ten and forty miles (16 and 64 km) from top to bottom,

> *"The chess-board is the world; the pieces are the phenomena of the universe; the rules of the game are what we call the Laws of Nature."*
>
> — T. H. Huxley

*Ultramafic rock are bits of the mantle that have been brought up to the surface by upwelling magma. Geologists study these rocks for clues to the composition of the planet's interior.*

## Deep-Sea Drilling

Scientists use a variety of methods to figure out what is going on beneath the Earth's surface. Much of their knowledge has been inferred from studying phenomena such as volcanic eruptions and seafloor spreading. However, a wealth of direct evidence of the composition of the earth's crust has come from deep-sea drilling carried out by the JOIDES *Resolution (below)*, which is operated by Texas A&M University. This scientific vessel carries enough drilling pipe to bore thousands of feet into the sediments and underlying basaltic crust. Sometimes the pipe has even brought up samples of mantle rock that has intruded into the crust.

but because the rock is mostly granite and granodiorite composed of lighter elements such as silicon and aluminum, they float higher on the mantle. The plates' movements as they diverge, converge, and slip past each other shape our visible world: Where they collide, mountains form and volcanoes erupt; where they pull apart, ocean basins form; where they grate against each other, earthquakes tear apart the crust.

### CONVECTION CURRENTS

Plate movement is believed to be produced by convection currents that flow in the mantle rock. It is hard to imagine rock moving, but that is exactly what may be happening: The burning-hot core heats mantle rock to temperatures exceeding 1,835°F (1,002°C) causing it to deform and move at an infinitesimally slow rate called creeping. As the mantle rock deforms, it rises, cools, and sinks, where it is reheated and rises again. It has been estimated that rock heated in this way would take fifty-eight million years to reach the top of the mantle from the bottom. While most scientists agree that convection is behind plate motion, no one is quite sure whether the convection takes place throughout the mantle's entire depth or just the top four hundred or so miles (640 or so km).

### WHERE THE PLATES MEET

Plate boundaries—where one plate meets another—are lively places. Sometimes two continental plates collide in a gigantic shoving match in which one plate crumples, resulting in the rise of an inland mountain range, such as the Himalayas. At other times, a continental plate pushes against an oceanic plate, and the continental plate forces the heavier oceanic plate downward in a process known as subduction. As the oceanic plate descends some forty to eighty miles (65 to 130 km), heat from the mantle melts a small fraction of the descending plate. The

**Continental Fit**
The existence of the same ancient crystalline rock (found in areas marked above) on South America and Africa and on North America and Europe is cited as evidence that the continents bordering the Atlantic Ocean once fit together like pieces of a puzzle.

the continents don't stay put—and never have. Some 250 million years ago, all of today's continents were part of one supercontinent called Pangaea. Pangaea was located in the southern hemisphere and featured long mountain ranges, an inner sea, and some glaciation. It was home to plants and animals, including the *Mesosaurus*, a marine reptile. But convection doomed this unbroken continental unit to division and endless wandering. Rifts opened and became inlets, seas, and eventually oceans. New crust poured from undersea rifts such as the Mid-Atlantic Ridge, pushing pieces of Pangaea apart.

Now continents are scattered over the globe, but geologists have managed to reconstruct much of the puzzle. By analyzing rocks, glacial scrapings, and fossils, they have demonstrated that the Appalachian mountain range of North America and the Caledonian range of Europe were once parts of the same mountain chain; that Florida once belonged to western Africa; and that Brazil once snuggled next to Nigeria.

resulting magma then rises through the overlying plate to create chains of coastal volcanoes, such as the Andes and Cascades. Subduction also occurs between oceanic plates.

California's San Andreas Fault is the site of a third type of boundary conflict. Here two plates slide against one another in opposite directions, producing tremors (and human anxiety), but no subduction.

Given all this activity on the surface of Earth, it's not surprising that

The discovery of fossils of the Glossopteris flora in South America, Africa, India, Australia, and Antarctica argues in favor of the theory that all these continents were once part of Gondwana, the southern land mass of the ancient supercontinent called Pangaea.

# "Utter, damned, rot!"

The idea that the outer part of the planet consists of enormous rigid plates that move over the surface of the globe is now accepted by scientists everywhere. But its status as a bedrock tenet of geology comes too late for Alfred Wegener, the German meteorologist who first formulated the theory of continental drift during the early years of this century. Wegener was roundly denounced and summarily dismissed. His hypothesis was treated as pure bunk—in the words of the president of the American Philosophical Society, "utter, damned, rot!"

## CONTINENTS ON THE MOVE

As early as the sixteenth century, observers had noted that North America and Europe looked as if they might have once been united. But without supporting evidence, this seemed merely coincidental. In 1912 Wegener, then a young teacher of physical sciences at University of Marburg, advanced a radical hypothesis. He suggested the continents were plates that moved around the surface of the Earth. His term for the movement was *die Verschiebung der Kontinente* (continental displacement). In the course of his own travels, Wegener had noticed similarities in age between glacial deposits in South Africa and South America. He also had found—on different continents—fossils that had once shared a common environment. And on one of his trips to Greenland he had noted that the land seemed to have shifted from the position scientists had recorded in 1823

and 1870. The continental drift hypothesis appealed to Wegener because it helped explain these anomalies and such things as the birth of mountains at the margins of continents.

From the time Wegener's theory was published in 1915 as *The Origin of Continents and Oceans* until his death in 1930 the work inspired ridicule. Supporters were few and far between—a notable exception was respected South African scientist Alexander Du Toit, who dedicated

*Since Alfred Wegener was neither a geologist nor a paleontologist, his new theory of continental drift—which affects how we look at many kinds of geological activity—was viewed with enormous suspicion by the establishment.*

**TWO HUNDRED MILLION YEARS AGO**

**ONE HUNDRED MILLION YEARS AGO**

**PRESENT**

**FIFTY MILLION YEARS IN THE FUTURE**

*Pangaea ("pan" = all, "gaia" = earth) was the name given by Alfred Wegener to what he supposed to be the mother of all existing continents. About two hundred million years ago Pangaea began to break up and Europe and Asia drifted north. Over the next one hundred million years, the Mid-Atlantic Ridge developed, dividing the Americas from Africa. Today the Atlantic Ocean separates North America from Europe and India has joined Asia. Based on modern observations of plate movements, the future holds equally dramatic changes, including the breaking away of Africa from Asia.*

his 1937 book *Our Wandering Continents* to Wegener. Despite his academic credentials in astronomy and meteorology and his reputation as a marvelous teacher, Wegener was repeatedly denied professorships.

Why did Wegener's theory arouse such hostility? Part of the reaction was due to his attempt to propose centrifugal force and gravity as possible engines of drift. But it was the flawed measurements Wegener took in Greenland—leading him to conclude erroneously

*The relentless movement of icebergs, observed by Wegener on a 1906 trip to Greenland, may have helped inspire his theory of continents on the move.*

that the land was moving at a rate of 118 feet per year—that really gave his detractors the ammunition they needed to debunk the theory. Even if Wegener's groundbreaking work had been flawless, it would probably have met strong opposition. As one scientist noted at a 1928 symposium held by the American Association of Petroleum Geologists: "If we are to believe Wegener's hypothesis, we must forget everything which has been learned in the last seventy years and start all over!"

# Volcanoes & Earthquakes

On May 18, 1980, after months of earthquakes and ventings, Washington's Mount St. Helens exploded with the force of twenty-five million tons of TNT. The event was a vivid reminder of the energies at work in plate tectonics.

From Pompeii to Pinatubo, volcanoes have visited extraordinary destruction on their surroundings. But only with the development of tectonic theory have we been able to really understand how these convulsions work. Nearly all volcanoes are concentrated along plate margins. In fact, the oceanic rift zones themselves constitute one continuous volcano, extruding magma and creating crust. One of them, the Mid-Atlantic Ridge, rises above sea level only in one place: Iceland. Other volcanic forms are closer to home—sometimes too close.

## MAGMA MOVEMENT

Sometimes the material near the top of the mantle liquifies to magma. Propelled by convection currents, jets of magma known as plumes rise into the crust and are injected into fractured sedimentary rock. There the magma cools, is exposed to weathering, and forms various rock formations such as squat plugs, finlike dikes, and flat sills.

When magma breaks through the surface, it is called lava. Depending on its chemistry, lava can either explode, as at Mount St. Helens, or flow like molasses, as on the island of Hawaii. Some lavas are so runny that they can flow for miles before forming mounded shield volcanoes

Fragmentary volcanic rock materials called pyroclasts lie on the slopes of Mount Vesuvius, a volcano that has erupted more than twenty times in the last four hundred years.

or layered plains of basalt, as in the case of the great Columbia Plateau.

When plumes melt continental crust, underground chambers of magma can erupt explosively. Sometimes this results in huge craters, or calderas, such as Oregon's Crater Lake. Some plumes form permanent hot spots in the mantle. They shoot holes through moving crust, creating volcanic chains. This is how the Emperor Seamounts, a volcanic chain that includes the Hawaiian Islands, was formed.

By far the most spectacular volcanoes are stratovolcanoes, those made of andesitic lava, a fine-grained volcanic rock crystallized from magma containing 60 percent silica. Such volcanoes rise to great heights. For example, at 22,834 feet (6,960 m), the stratovolcano Aconcagua in the Argentine Andes is the tallest peak in the western hemisphere. Like Mount Fuji and such Cascade Range peaks as Mount St. Helens, it is a towering cone built of alternating layers of tephra (cinder, pumice, and fine ash) and lava flows.

Stratovolcanoes originate in subduction. When sinking oceanic crust passes beneath a continen-

*The ash cloud produced by the 1980 eruption of Mount St. Helens brought darkness at noon to areas more than 150 miles (240 km) away and deposited ash up to four inches (10 cm) deep on much of Washington, northern Idaho, and western Montana.*

*Tectonic plates that meet along the seven-hundred-mile-long (1,100 km) San Andreas Fault in California grind past each other at an average rate of 1.5 inches (4 cm) a year, producing tiny earthquakes on a regular basis. In some areas, however, the plates lock until pressure builds and forces them apart, triggering a huge earthquake such as the one that devastated San Francisco in 1906.*

tal plate, it partially melts, creating magma, which works its way to the surface. Subduction zones, the most famous being the Pacific Ring of Fire, are rimmed with stratovolcanoes. Their massive explosions make history. It is said that ash particles from the 1883 explosion of Krakatoa, between Java and Sumatra, drifted as far as England and explain why the seascapes of the painter J. M. W. Turner are infused with hazy golden light.

**TURBULENT PLATE MARGINS**
More than a million earthquakes rattle the planet every year. Almost all are too slight to be felt but they register on seismographs, allowing us to pinpoint locations and understand the phenomenon's function. Like volcanoes, major earthquakes tend to shadow the plate margins on land and in the sea along the mid-oceanic ridges, where new crust is forming. Scientists now believe these regions are wide zones of almost constant stretching and compressing driven by convection currents.

In an earthquake, rock is compressed and deformed, then broken, releasing pent-up energy, which nudges the plates into a new position. Scientists have measured displacement of up to forty-five feet in a single surge—enough to move a house across a city street.

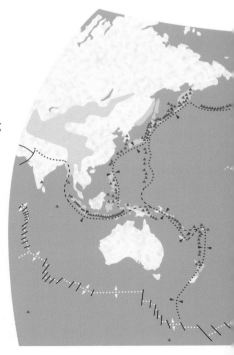

An earthquake's actual point of tension release is called the focus and the point on the surface directly above the focus is called the epicenter. Energy radiates outward from the focus in all directions. Primary (P) and secondary (S) waves cause the ground to shake, buckle, subside, or shift. Undersea earthquakes send seismic waves through water, and when these reach shallow coastal shelves they can be strong enough to cause destructive hundred-foot-high (30 m) waves, or tsunamis.

Fault zones, areas of weakness in the rock caused by plate movement, are numerous along plate margins, and in locations such as California they influence everything from coastlines to insurance rates. Faults themselves describe fractures in the zones, and they are defined by the relative movement of the crust at the fracture. The crust can move above the fault plane (the surface along which the rock fractured), or below. It can also move right or left. In a so-called normal fault, the crustal rock sinks down in relation to rock above. With a reverse fault, the crust moves up in relation to rock below, sometimes bringing older rock to rest on top of younger rock. And at a transform or strike-slip faults, two pieces of crust slip past one another, as happens periodically in the San Andreas Fault.

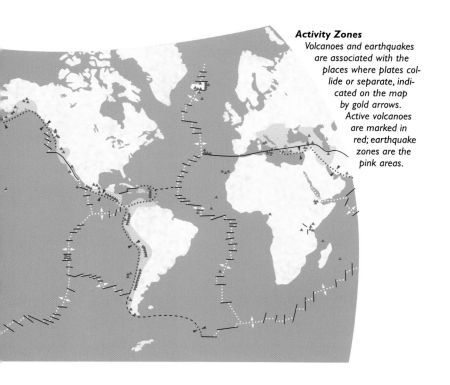

**Activity Zones**
Volcanoes and earthquakes are associated with the places where plates collide or separate, indicated on the map by gold arrows. Active volcanoes are marked in red; earthquake zones are the pink areas.

# Weather & Erosion

Although synonymous with solidity, rock does not last forever on the surface of the Earth. It is constantly being broken down into smaller physical and chemical constituents by weathering, and is then eroded, or carried away by rains, rivers, and other forces.

Exposure is key to weathering. Factors such as temperature change cause rocks to expand and contract, creating fissures. Invading rainwater freezes and expands, splitting them further. Tree roots and animal burrows enlarge cracks, letting in still more water.

With enough unmelted snow, glaciers develop, gouging out dramatic U-shaped valleys and grinding rock down into what's called glacial flour. It is this material, covering about an eighth of Earth's surface, that turns lakes and streams turquoise-green. If glaciers scour away enough crust, they can uncover many types of rock, including massive underground

*Weathering has shaped unusual sandstone rock formations in the Painted Desert in northeastern Arizona.*

bodies of granite called batholiths. When the pressure from above is released, batholiths "unload" into great domes, sometimes cracking and shedding layers like an onion in a process known as exfoliation.

Gravity adds to the weathering process, turning running water into a saw that cuts though strata. Once

*Weathering sculpted the curved surface of this granite boulder.*

the water reaches the ocean, it continues to pound away at rock. Wave action cuts coves in stern coastlines, hollowing out arches that collapse into stacks. In arid regions, sedimentary rock is broken apart by growing salt crystals. Sand grains carried on desert winds blast away at parent strata, carving spires and hoodoos and depositing restless sand dunes. The spectacle of physical weathering and erosion can be an awe-inspiring sight. On the Colorado Plateau in Arizona, home to Monument Valley and the Grand Canyon, more than a vertical mile (1.6 km) of sedimentary rock has been removed by water and wind.

## CHEMICAL WEATHERING

Rocks formed under heat and pressure become unstable in the cooler world of the surface and are ripe for chemical reorganization. Water is the chief agent of change. As rain, it gathers carbon dioxide from the atmosphere and falls as carbonic acid. Though weak, the acid hollows out caves in limestone. Through hydrolysis and leaching, water changes the basic chemistry of rock. When hydrogen ions enter feldspar, for instance, they take the place of potassium ions, changing the feldspar to a clay called kaolinite.

But water is not the only agent of chemical change. Mosses and lichens produce organic acids that reduce the cohesion of rock, as anyone who owns a stone wall will attest. Even air works change upon rock. Oxygen reacts with the iron in rocks to produce iron oxide, seen as a reddish rust or a varnish.

The reduction of rock makes life on Earth possible through the creation of soil. This blend of unconsolidated rocks and organic matter provides a home for plants and microorganisms. Chemical weathering is known to increase the concentration of valuable minerals such as iron, nickel, and manganese. And in the case of gold loosed from mountain batholiths and washed into river deposits, weathering and erosion can be extremely profitable.

*Patches of lichen eat away at the stone of this statue.*

# AN ENDLESS CYCLE

*The rocks that compose the Earth's crust are constantly being recycled in a process that spans hundreds of millions of years.*

When it comes to nature, we are accustomed to thinking in cycles. We look upon weather as part of a hydrologic cycle, where water renews itself through phases of condensation and evaporation. In organic life, nutrients are recycled through digestion and decay. Rocks, too, march to this drummer. They and their constituent minerals are constantly changing form in a prescribed pattern traced in the rock cycle diagram on the opposite page. This cycle summarizes the relationship between the different rock forms:

*"...the recycling of the earth's materials is a subplot in a dramatic story that begins with dark scums in motion..."*

— John McPhee

igneous, sedimentary, and metamorphic. Not all rocks proceed through each step, however. The cycle merely describes the possible avenues of change that rock can follow. And as with all cycles, there is, in the words of the eighteenth-century geologist James Hutton, "no vestige of a beginning—no prospect of an end."

### FROM MAGMA TO ROCK
The cycle is best understood by starting with the formation of igneous rock from magma. When magma pours out of the Earth from volca-

## "The Present is the Key to the Past"

James Hutton (1726-1797), regarded as the father of modern geology, devoted himself to the study of landforms around his native Edinburgh, Scotland. Patient observation of deformed and tilted strata led him to conclude that rock is constantly being thrust up from the sea and worn down by weathering—processes he viewed as primordial and destined to continue ad infinitum. He realized that the geological forces we see at work around us are the same forces that shaped the past. In his words, "the present is the key to the past." His ideas were considered revolutionary, even blasphemous: When he published his groundbreaking book *Theory of the Earth* in 1795, most Europeans held to a literal interpretation of Christian theology that placed the origin of Earth in the year 4004 B.C.

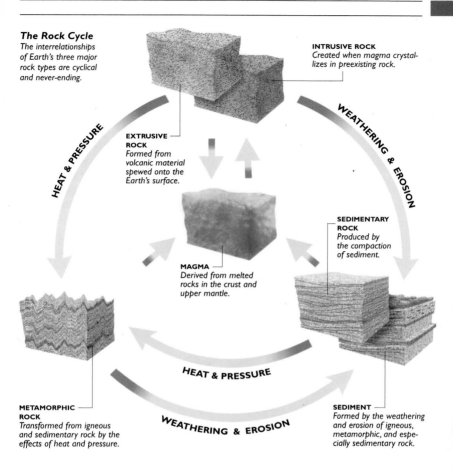

**The Rock Cycle**
*The interrelationships of Earth's three major rock types are cyclical and never-ending.*

**INTRUSIVE ROCK**
*Created when magma crystallizes in preexisting rock.*

**EXTRUSIVE ROCK**
*Formed from volcanic material spewed onto the Earth's surface.*

**HEAT & PRESSURE**

**WEATHERING & EROSION**

**SEDIMENTARY ROCK**
*Produced by the compaction of sediment.*

**MAGMA**
*Derived from melted rocks in the crust and upper mantle.*

**HEAT & PRESSURE**

**METAMORPHIC ROCK**
*Transformed from igneous and sedimentary rock by the effects of heat and pressure.*

**WEATHERING & EROSION**

**SEDIMENT**
*Formed by the weathering and erosion of igneous, metamorphic, and especially sedimentary rock.*

noes and dikes, it hardens rapidly as extrusive (volcanic) igneous rock; when it crystallizes beneath the surface, it is known as intrusive (plutonic) igneous rock. Over time, wind and rain can reduce all rock to sediment, including deeply buried intrusive rock, which is first exposed by erosion. Chemical bonding and pressure from above compact the sediment, transforming, or lithifying, it into sedimentary rock.

Weathering and erosion affect and change all rock, not just

igneous rock. And the changes don't stop there. Extremely high heat and pressure can gradually alter all rocks into another rock— metamorphic rock.

The full circle is completed when rocks—of all kinds—are buried deep enough for the heat of the Earth's core to melt them into magma once again. This can happen when tectonic plates collide along a plate margin *(page 16)*. One plate slips down under another, and is buried deeply.

# Rock from the Deep

Igneous rock forms when magma—molten rock from the Earth's mantle—cools and hardens. Where and how fast the magma cools, as well as its mineral composition, determine what kind of igneous rock it becomes. Thus the different types of igneous rock are usually classified either by their origin or by their chemical composition.

Because of its primary mineral constituents, feldspar and quartz, granite is a very hard rock that resists weathering—a perfect stone for constructing buildings and carving sculptures.

Rocks born of volcanoes, vents, or ocean-floor rifts are extrusive (volcanic) igneous rocks. The minerals that form these rocks don't crystallize until they reach the surface of the Earth. Once out in the air or water, they cool quickly—too fast, in fact, for large crystals to form. Basalt is the most common extrusive igneous rock. Its texture is so fine-grained—its crystals are less than 0.64 inch (1.6 cm) in size—that the crystals can't be seen without a microscope.

Obsidian, another extrusive rock, forms so rapidly when lava hits the air that it never has a chance to develop the crystal lattices that are typical of most minerals. This is a rock that looks and feels like glass.

Igneous rocks such as granite and pegmatite are also born of molten rock, but they cool slowly underground. There is thus enough time for larger crystals to form before the material hardens. These rocks are classified as intrusive (plutonic) igneous rocks, and they are created when heat melts the underside of a continent or a piece of sinking ocean crust. The magma rises in enormous blobs, cooling and crystallizing as it goes. A blob, or pluton, comes to rest in the crust before it reaches the surface. Eons later, when weathering has removed overlying layers of older rock, the intrusive rock appears—like a new tooth erupting through a gum.

Intrusive rock structures take on many shapes and sizes. The largest are batholiths, and the largest of

The dark areas visible on this piece of granite indicate the presence of hornblende, a common mineral that is found in both igneous and metamorphic rocks.

As basalt cools, it commonly contracts into hexagonal columns along the seams of its chemical bonds. In Northern Ireland, the Giant's Causeway is an endless dike of broken basalt stepping-stones—each a six-sided form—reaching all the way to Scotland.

these form huge mountain ranges. California's Sierra Nevada range is a batholith measuring about four hundred miles (640 km) long and eighty miles (130 km) wide. The landscape known so well to visitors is solid granite, and the wonders they hike to see, such as Half Dome in Yosemite National Park, are eroded intrusives.

### MINERAL MAKEUP

The mineral building blocks of igneous rocks are typically feldspars, ferro-magnesians, micas, and quartzes. Since the element silica is their primary ingredient, all these minerals are known as silicates. As the content of silica varies, the consistency of the magma changes. Lava from magma with little silica can be very runny—in Hawaii, it often flows at speeds of thirty-five miles (56 km) per hour. A higher silica content creates more viscous rock such as the football-sized volcanic bombs or the blocky-crusty flows called "Aa." And when lava contains a great deal of silica and carbon dioxide, it explodes in a violent volcanic eruption.

### Telltale Signs

The first clue to the identity of a common igneous rock is its locality: Look for signs of volcanism: dikes, sills, and, of course, volcanoes. Other clues include:

• Color: The lighter the color, the higher the silica content. A light-colored rock (65 percent silica) may be granite, pegmatite, or rhyolite. A medium-colored rock (55 to 65 percent silica) may be gabbro or andesite. A dark-colored rock (45 to 55 percent silica) may be basalt, serpentinite, or peridotite.

• Granular Texture: The size of a rock's mineral grains can help in narrowing possibilities. Coarse-grained rocks (grains visible to the eye) include granite, granidiorite, pegmatite, nepheline syenite, and gabbro. Fine-grained rocks (invisible grains) include basalt, rhyolite, and andesite.

# Rock from Sediments

Sedimentary rock is the Earth's greatest storyteller. This type of rock forms in layers, and the order

The imposing white cliffs that run along England's southern coast are made of chalk, a soft sedimentary limestone that is gradually eroding into the English Channel.

in which these layers are laid down—their sequence—recounts the geologic history of the region. The archetypal recycled rock, sedimentary rock is made from sediment produced by the breakdown of other rocks—mostly other sedimentary rock, but also igneous and metamorphic rock.

Although sedimentary rock makes up only about 5 percent of all the rock in the Earth's crust, it accounts for 75 percent of what you see on the surface. That's because the rock originates there. Wind, rain, snow, and ice reduce existing rock to particles, carrying the sediments far and wide. In time, the sediments come to rest in layers, also called beds or strata. Here they are pressed, squeezed,

and changed into rock through a process known as lithification. Minerals of various kinds, including calcite, quartz, and iron oxide, cement the layers.

**LARGE AND SMALL**
If they are washed out to sea, sediments cover the continental shelves, slip into canyons, and spread across the ocean floor in huge undersea sandstorms, called turbidity flows. Along the way, the sediments are sorted out according to their size, shape, and weight. The smaller, lighter, and more rounded a particle is, the more likely it will be deposited far out to sea. Heavier

Breccia is a sedimentary rock containing fragments of any type of igneous, metamorphic, or sedimentary rock set in a fine-grained matrix.

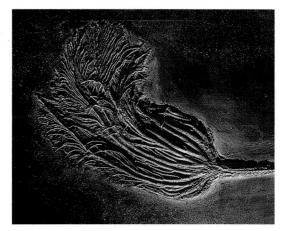

A marine fossil, such as a crinoid, indicates that the rock was formed from seafloor sediment.

particles are deposited closer to shore. When panning for gold, prospectors employ small-scale turbidity currents, sorting out the lightweight sediments and looking for the heavier gold at the bottom of the pan.

Geologists classify sedimentary rocks by the size of their grains. At one extreme lies shale, a fine-grained mudstone that accounts for 80 percent of the sedimentary rock in the world. At the other end of the scale are the chunky, coarse-grained conglomerates, which form where water currents are powerful enough to move large rock fragments.

Some sedimentary rocks form by chemical precipitation. For instance, limestone, formed mostly in oceans and lakes, is created by the precipitation of calcium carbonate from seawater or shelly skeletons of marine organisms. The precipitate accumulates, then is lithified into limestone strata. When the strata are uplifted, weathering dissolves the calcium carbonate and it is redeposited in fissures and caves in a variety of shapes, including stalagmites and stalactites.

Bituminous coal is another sedimentary rock. It forms from plants and animals that have decomposed in swamps. Over time, these fine sediments are compressed. The deeper the deposit, the harder and purer the coal, and the cleaner and more slowly it burns. The purest form of coal is anthracite, once bituminous coal but altered by pressure until it became another rock.

## Telltale Signs

Identifying characteristics of sedimentary rock include:

- Fossil Content: If the rock contains fossils, it's a sure sign that it is a sedimentary rock. (Only rarely does metamorphic rock contain fossils.) Furthermore, the type of fossil can tell you something about the rock's origin.
- Grain Size: Grains in sedimentary rock can range from boulders to microscopic particles of clay. The grain size helps distinguish one sedimentary rock from another. Fine-grained rock includes clays and mudstones, such as shales. Medium-grained rock includes sandstones and graywacke. Coarse-grained rock includes conglomerates and breccias.

# Geodes

Step into the mineralogy section of a museum or a rock collector's shop and your eye will immediately light on the geodes. Resistance is futile. These are among the most enchanting—and puzzling—of Earth's creations.

There are conflicting views about how geodes form, but most geologists agree that they begin as bubbles—sometimes in submarine limestone sediments, sometimes in a lava flow. Occasionally they form around the body of a sea creature on the ocean floor. Over time, the bubble is cast in a hard shell of silica, and water containing dissolved material is trapped inside. The precipitate that results is composed of a variety of minerals, usually quartz or calcite, but also aragonite, magnetite, barite, and chalcopyrite. Many thousands of years later, weathering lifts the hard little silica orb away from the surrounding rock.

The exterior of the sphere appears dull and pitted, which is no doubt why the Greeks called them *geoides*, meaning "earthlike." However, on the inside, they can look heavenly. The precipitate forms a lining of inward projecting crystals and, since different minerals harden at varying temperatures, the material forms layers.

Sometimes a cavity may be completely filled by layers. Purists refer to these geodes as nodules. Crack open a nodule and instead of a hollow crystalline core, you might find haloes of brilliantly hued agate, produced where chalcedony-laden water precipitated within the shell.

## COLLECTOR'S PASSION

Whether transparent or smoky, blue or or gold, geodes have long been favorites of collectors. The thrill of beholding one is surpassed only by the excitement of finding one. The best locations to look are in deserts—the western states, especially Arizona, Utah, and Nevada are popular hunting grounds. California's Riverside and Imperial counties are par-

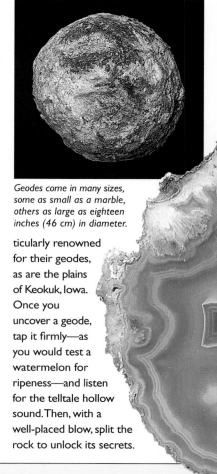

Geodes come in many sizes, some as small as a marble, others as large as eighteen inches (46 cm) in diameter.

ticularly renowned for their geodes, as are the plains of Keokuk, Iowa. Once you uncover a geode, tap it firmly—as you would test a watermelon for ripeness—and listen for the telltale hollow sound. Then, with a well-placed blow, split the rock to unlock its secrets.

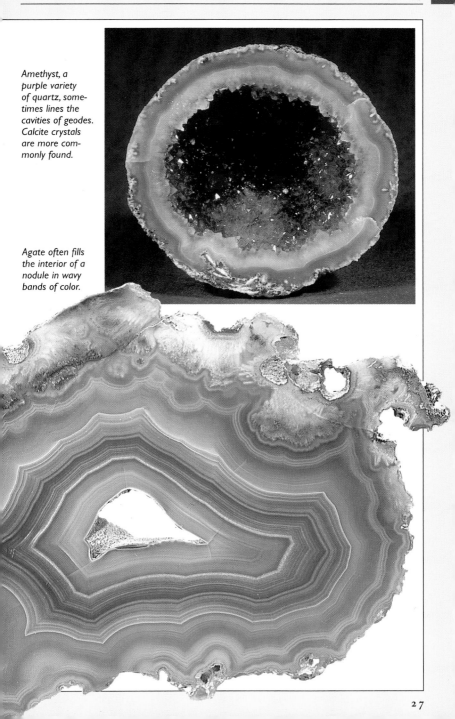

Amethyst, a purple variety of quartz, sometimes lines the cavities of geodes. Calcite crystals are more commonly found.

Agate often fills the interior of a nodule in wavy bands of color.

27

# Changed Rock

Metamorphic is the name given to rocks that have been transformed—made into totally different rocks. The change is wrought by heat and pressure so intense that the original rock's crystal structure alters without the rock ever leaving its solid state. The rock's minerals actually recrystallize without having melted first, the way they do when igneous rock forms from magma.

### AGENTS OF CHANGE

The heat that can transform rock is frequently produced by magma. When magma pushes up into colder continental rock, it heats up those rocks to a temperature approaching 900°F (480°C), baking their ingredients into new arrange-

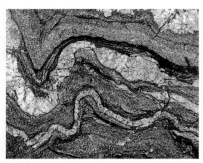

*The foliation evident on this coarse-grained migmatite indicates it is a regional metamorphic rock that was created at high temperatures and pressures.*

ments. If granitic magma, for example, intrudes into limestone, the magma's heat causes the primary mineral in limestone—calcite—to recrystallize. The end result is marble. Geologists call this process contact metamorphism. Shales, mudstones, and impure limestones are susceptible to transformation in this way.

Pressure, another agent of change, is produced by the weight of the covering rocks or the movement of the tectonic plates, particularly along plate margins. When plates collide, rock may be compressed like an accordion until it forms mountains. The increased pressure on the rock creates the heat necessary to rearrange the

## Telltale Signs

Common metamorphic rock can be identified by a variety of characteristics. Here are some things to look for:

• Foliation: Pressure forces certain crystals to align during the metamorphosis. The crystals look like they have been arranged in a linear pattern. Foliated rocks include slate, phyllite, schist, gneiss, amphibolite, and migmatite. Nonfoliated rocks include marble, quartzite, hornfels, and anthracite.

• Minerals Present: The presence of certain minerals—such as chlorite, pyrite, garnet, kyanite, and staurolite—are clues that a rock may be metamorphic. Chlorite and pyrite grow in slate and garnet; kyanite and staurolite occur in gneiss and schists.

• Grain Size: The higher the temperature that caused the rock to change from its original existence, the coarser the grain size. Gneiss is coarse-grained, schist is medium-grained, and slate is fine-grained.

*A regional metamorphic rock, slate is usually derived from shales under conditions of low temperature and pressure. It is so fine-grained that its individual minerals—such as quartz, feldspar, mica, and chlorite—cannot be seen without a microscope.*

Metamorphosis usually occurs over a very long period of time, but occasionally it is almost instantaneous, as in the case of lightning striking sand and transforming it into the rock known as fulgurite.

Sometimes change continues beyond the original metamorphosis. Pressure can transform sedimentary shale to metamorphic slate, but if the pressure is sustained the slate goes on to become phyllite, and then mica schist. With each change, the crystals grow larger, eventually producing the wavy bands characteristic of mica schist.

crystals so that they all align in the same direction, perpendicular to the direction of the pressure. This recrystallization process is referred to as regional metamorphism. Granite, when folded and heated in this manner, becomes gneiss, a rock that is often identified by its banded or foliated appearance.

Both contact and regional metamorphism not only rearrange crystals, but also squeeze water out and make rocks denser and harder. Some of Earth's hardest materials are formed this way, including quartzite (often confused with marble) and the gemstones— emeralds, rubies, and jades.

*Under the hands of a true artist, marble comes alive, as in this pietà by Michelangelo.*

# Cosmic Rock

Earth takes thousands of body blows every year from extraterrestrial objects. Some of these rocks from outer space weigh a few ounces, others are big enough to leave permanent scars. In Manicouagan, Quebec, for example, a meteorite struck Earth two hundred million years ago, creating a crater that measures forty-three miles (69 km) across. But an even more lasting impact is the way these meteorites can alter life itself. Many scientists now believe that an extraterrestrial object, perhaps a comet or more likely an asteroid, smashed into Earth about sixty-five million years ago off what is now Mexico's Yucatan Peninsula. Some evidence suggests that the object may have been about ten miles (16 km) in diameter, creating an impact that rocked the planet and changed the climate so drastically that the dinosaurs became extinct.

*Discovered in 1920 in Hoba, Namibia, this iron meteorite measures about ten feet (3 m) by three feet (1 m) and weighs thirty tons.*

## FREQUENT VISITORS

Rock bombardment was far more intense in the early days of the solar system. At that time, huge bodies of molten nickel-iron alloy consolidated to form planets. Others became asteroids. Today more than a hundred thousand asteroids circle the sun in an asteroid belt located between the planets Mars and Jupiter. When asteroids collide, chunks of material are

knocked off, or the bodies may careen out of orbit. Some come rocketing toward Earth.

Most such interplanetary bodies shatter or explode as they pass through Earth's atmosphere. Those that stay intact and reach the surface of the planet are called meteorites. The bright flash that each one makes as it zooms across the night sky, often called a shooting star, is more correctly termed a meteor.

Meteorites can be divided into three different groups according to their mineral makeup: iron, stony-iron, and stony.

They contain the same minerals as the core and mantle of our planet. Iron meteorites, much like the core, are composed of an alloy of nickel and iron. Stony-iron meteorites contain pyroxene as well as the nickel-iron alloy. And stony meteorites, which make up more than 80 percent of all cosmic rocks, are mainly olivine and pyroxene, with only a hint of iron-nickel alloy. Certain stony meteorites contain organic compounds, leading some scientists to ponder the intrigueing idea that life itself may have originally arrived on Earth via airmail.

*Tektites are rocks made of both terrestrial and extraterrestrial materials. They are created when a meteor hits Earth, producing such heat that bits of both the meteor and Earth rock melt, shoot up in the air, and combine in a molten mass, sometimes called a melt droplet, which then cools and falls to Earth.*

*The meteorite that made the three-quarter-mile-wide (1.2 km) Barringer Meteor Crater in northern Arizona probably weighed about two hundred thousand tons when it hit Earth some twenty-five thousand years ago.*

# ROCK RECORDS

*Dating methods such as stratigraphy and radiometry
serve as tools to decipher Earth's history.*

The record of rock is the song of Earth's history. Until the 1800s, that history was widely considered to be brief. Most people in Europe believed sixteenth-century Anglo-Irish Bishop James Ussher's contention that Earth was created in 4004 B.C. and had changed relatively little since its birth. But the work of several nineteenth-century scientists confounded that world view.

**REVOLUTIONARY THINKERS**

A key breakthrough in the study of Earth was made by James Hutton, a Scotsman who suggested that the history of rocks occurs in cycles *(page 20)*. Hutton argued that the scale of time for Earth's history was much greater than previously thought, because the weathering of rock from one form to another takes far longer than just a few thousand years.

Hutton's work was complemented by the observations of the English surveyor William Smith, who noticed that sedimentary layers of rock, also called beds or strata, occur in the same sequence throughout England. He concluded that the strata were deposited in chronological order, with the lower strata being the older ones.

One of the leading champions of the Scotsman's theories was Charles

*Charles Lyell (1797-1875) was a strong supporter of James Hutton's theories and took them even farther. He talked of the history of the planet in terms of millions of years.*

Lyell, who endorsed Hutton's view that geological events in the past occurred at the same rate as they do today—very, very slowly, for the most part.

## STRATIGRAPHY

The idea that the rock we see around us has been laid down in strata over many millions of years is the basis of stratigraphy. Geologists read strata like the lines of a book to gain an understanding of Earth's past. The location, thick-

*"...at every moment of past time Nature has added a page to her archives."*

— Sir Charles Lyell

ness, texture, color, and chemistry of the strata tell them where winds blew, waters flowed, and mountains rose. Entombed in many strata are the fossils of living things. Geologists use so-called index fossils—certain fossils associated with

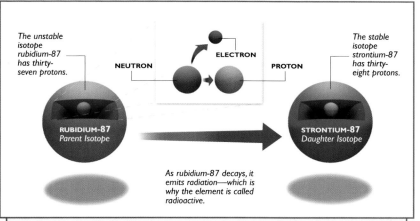

The unstable isotope rubidium-87 has thirty-seven protons.

**NEUTRON**

**ELECTRON**

**PROTON**

The stable isotope strontium-87 has thirty-eight protons.

**RUBIDIUM-87**
*Parent Isotope*

**STRONTIUM-87**
*Daughter Isotope*

As rubidium-87 decays, it emits radiation—which is why the element is called radioactive.

## Radioactive Decay

All rocks contain radioactive elements such as uranium and rubidium. The atomic nuclei of these elements are unstable, and over time they naturally decay into the more stable nuclei of a different element. Such variable forms are called isotopes *(page 47)*. Scientists call the unstable atoms "parents" and the more stable atoms "daughters." One of the ways a parent isotope changes into a daughter isotope is by emitting an electron (a negative charge) from a neutron, thereby converting the neutron to a proton (a positive charge). The daughter isotope now has one more proton. This is how rubidium-87 changes into strontium-87.

Parents decay into daughters at a fixed rate that is particular to that element. Scientists measure these rates in half-lives: that is, the time it takes for half of the parents in a sample to decay. This process can take minutes or billions of years—depending on the element. Using a sensitive instrument called a mass spectrometer, scientists tally the number of newly formed daughters and the number of remaining parents in a given rock. Then, knowing the decay rate, they can count backwards to when the radioactive clock began to tick and figure out how long ago the rock was formed—a time when there were no daughters, only parents.

## MAJOR METHODS OF DATING ROCKS

| METHOD | TYPES OF ROCKS | EFFECTIVE DATING RANGE |
|---|---|---|
| *RADIOMETRY* | | |
| **CARBON-14** | Sedimentary rock | 70 thousand years or less |
| **POTASSIUM-ARGON** | Igneous rock, especially basalt | 5 thousand years or more |
| **RUBIDIUM-STRONTIUM** | Igneous rock, especially granite | 5 million years or more |
| **URANIUM-LEAD** | Igneous, sedimentary, and metamorphic rock | 10 million years or more |
| *STRATIGRAPHY* | | |
| **INDEX FOSSILS** | Sedimentary rock | 700 million years or less |
| **PALEOMAGNETISM** | Igneous rock, especially basalt, and some sedimentary rock | 3 billion years or less |

*The chart above shows some of the most common tests used to determine the age of a rock. To ensure accuracy, geologists will use different tests on a single sample. Radiometric dating methods can give the absolute age of certain rocks. Stratigraphy can tell the relative age of one rock when compared to another rock.*

particular periods in geologic history—to help date the surrounding strata. By knowing which fossils belong together, scientists can reconstruct the original pattern of the strata—even where faulting has disturbed sediments and jumbled strata.

As important as stratigraphy is, it only reveals the relative age of a layer of one rock with respect to another layer. Fortunately, in the last century scientists have unlocked the workings of Earth's inner clock. By looking at the decay of radioactive elements *(box, page 33)*, geologists now can tell when a rock was formed. For example, the radiometric technique known as potassium-argon dating reveals when lavas and magmas cooled. The method called rubidium-strontium dating has pinpointed the age of granitic gneiss in Greenland at 3.8 billion years. Radiometry has even been used to date moon rock at 4.6 billion years.

Dating by radioactive decay can be used for all types of rock, but it is most often used with igneous rock. For some sedimentary rock as well as igneous rock, geologists also use paleomagnetic dating methods.

### PALEOMAGNETISM

Earth's core is a geodynamo: The inner and outer cores spin at different rates—possibly even in different directions—creating a magnetic field. Igneous rocks, particularly basalt, acquire a magnetic fingerprint—a structural alignment with Earth's magnetic field—when they first crystallize. The rock retains that print forever—unless it remelts to magma.

What makes this particularly relevant to geochronologists is that in the 1960s scientists discovered that Earth's magnetic polarity has changed numerous times throughout history, with magnetic north becoming magnetic south and vice versa. Such reversals have occurred on average about every seven thousand centuries—each transition lasting from a few thousand years to about 1.4 million years.

This knowledge came in especially handy when scientists were looking for evidence that plate tectonics was indeed behind the formation of the Mid-Atlantic Ridge. Using paleomagnetic dating techniques, they discovered submarine basalt stripes of differing magnetic polarity paired symmetrically on either side of the rift. By radiometric dating, the scientists were able to determine that the farther away from the ridge the stripe was—on either side—the older the rock. Taken together, this data suggested that new crust is constantly being created at the edges of the plate in conveyor-belt fashion by the movement of Earth's plates.

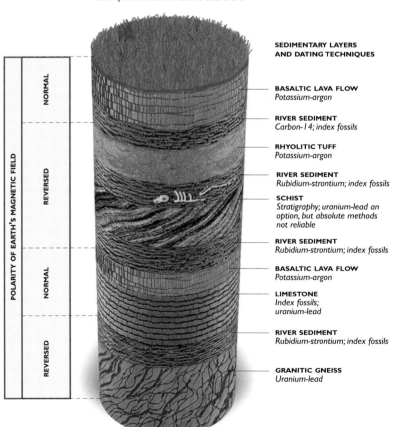

**Pillar of Time**
This illustration represents an idealized sample taken from Earth's crust, depicting a range of possible strata and the techniques that can be used to date them.

SEDIMENTARY LAYERS
AND DATING TECHNIQUES

BASALTIC LAVA FLOW
Potassium-argon

RIVER SEDIMENT
Carbon-14; index fossils

RHYOLITIC TUFF
Potassium-argon

RIVER SEDIMENT
Rubidium-strontium; index fossils

SCHIST
Stratigraphy; uranium-lead an option, but absolute methods not reliable

RIVER SEDIMENT
Rubidium-strontium; index fossils

BASALTIC LAVA FLOW
Potassium-argon

LIMESTONE
Index fossils; uranium-lead

RIVER SEDIMENT
Rubidium-strontium; index fossils

GRANITIC GNEISS
Uranium-lead

POLARITY OF EARTH'S MAGNETIC FIELD

NORMAL

REVERSED

NORMAL

REVERSED

# Deep Time

Science views time on scales both very small and very large. At one end of the spectrum, physicists discuss events that take trillionths of a second. At the other, astronomers and geologists are preoccupied with deep time—time that is measured in millions or billions of years. An astronomer looking at a galaxy may be seeing what it looked like billions of years ago. A geologist reading the strata in the Grand Canyon is interpreting events that occurred over a period of two billion years. Because such numbers are almost impossible to comprehend, scientists sometimes metaphorically represent all of Earth's history as taking place in a year. If the planet was formed January 1st, life appeared in the oceans sometime in May, the dinosaurs in December, and humans in the last few seconds before midnight on New Year's Eve.

## RELATIVE VERSUS ABSOLUTE

For the geologist, there are two ways of looking at time: relative time, which embraces the sequence of events that formed the rock; and absolute time, which provides the actual age of the rock in years.

By the beginning of the twentieth century, geologists had developed a relative geologic time scale using the fundamental principles of stratigraphy: the law of horizontality, which dictates that sedimentary rock generally forms in horizontal layers; and the law of superposition, which holds that layers are older as they are deeper. Using these laws, they were able to correlate rock formations around the world and assemble a chronological record of the planetary past, dividing it into time units known as eons, eras, periods, and epochs.

Following the discovery of radioactivity at the end of the last century, radiometric dates were added to the

*During the nineteenth century, the history of Earth was encoded into a hierarchical scale of time units of varying duration. The hierarchy is known as the Stratigraphic Column.*

*Uluru Rock, also known as Ayers Rock, in Central Australia is estimated to be six hundred million years old.*

*New volcanic rock, called pahoehoe, is constantly being created in Hawaii.*

*Radiometric dating has placed the formation of this piece of graywacke taken from the Canadian Shield in the Precambrian period—more than 570 million years ago.*

relative geologic time scale. Now we know the absolute age of rocks around the world, from 3.5 billion-year-old rock in Australia and 3.8 billion-year-old rock in Greenland to the oldest exposed rock to be radiometrically dated—a 3.9 billion-year-old gneiss in Canada's Northwest Territories. Prior to its metamorphosis, this gneiss was a granite with its own life history. But radiometric dating techniques can only date rock to its last recrystallization, not to the original fire that created its building blocks.

*The granite walls of Colorado's Pikes Peak were formed about a billion years ago.*

# Fossils

Whatever we know about life in the prehistoric past is known because of fossils. They offer a peek at forms of life—dinosaurs, for instance—that no longer exist. But they also reveal much about rocks.

Fossils are fragmentary remains of plants or animals preserved in sedimentary rock (and a few other places). A fossil can be a hard shell, a bony skeleton, or a tooth. It can also be an imprint of an activity, such as a footprint. Or, it may even be an impression of the whole creature—mineralized. Few animals or plants end up as fossils. Usually they're eaten where they die by scavengers or bacteria. But anything buried before it decays or is consumed has a chance to be petrified.

Most fossils are located in limestones or fine-grained shales and mudstones, but some are found in ice, tar pits, or organic resin, called amber. These fossils generally don't undergo the wear and tear of those cast in rock and tend to be better preserved. Mammoths unearthed in Siberian permafrost still had fur and flesh on their bones.

Even so, sedimentary materials such as the fine limey muds of China have yielded fossil reptiles with the delicate imprints of feathers. And Canada's Burgess Shales formed so fast that even soft worms were preserved and later mineralized into iron pyrite.

### Windows into the Past

Amber has been used in jewelry for thousands of years, especially along the Baltic Sea, where deposits are plentiful. In the Middle Ages, the amber trade stretched all the way through Russia to the Black Sea. Amber formed anywhere from 360 to 3 million years ago when resinous sap from conifers and some flowering plants hardened and became fossilized. Its value is often enhanced by what it sometimes contains: fossilized pollens, flowers, and insects. The termite shown above became trapped in the gooey sap. The sap hardened, preserving the insect down to the last microscopic leg hair. Since tiny life forms rarely survive fossilization in rock, such amber fossils are treasured as windows into the past.

*A Slow Transformation*
*All marine fossils form in much the same way: The organism dies, is buried, and then is petrified.*

**PHASE ONE**
*The dead bodies of marine animals or plants sink to the bottom of the sea or lake. If they have soft tissue, it is eaten or rubbed away.*

Fossils of brachiopods are used as index fossils. Those shown here were uncovered in Franklin County, Indiana, in sedimentary rock formed some 440 million years ago.

Occasionally, when water saturated with silica percolates through the rock and fills the space once occupied by the organism, a gemstone called an opal forms. The result is a happy accident that may command hundreds of thousands of dollars from a collector, or—like the opalized pliosaur fossil that now resides in Sydney's Australian Museum—become a national treasure.

Geologists use fossils they call index fossils to date the sedimentary rock strata that contain them. Animals or plants that spread widely but had a relatively short tenure on Earth are the most useful for this. When paleontologists discover the fossilized remains of a trilobite, for example, they know immediately that the surrounding rock may date to the Cambrian period, some five hundred million years ago.

Where index fossils are not available, geologists rely on fossil assemblages. These are groups of fossils that are known to have lived during the same period, such as dinosaurs, redwoods, and dragonflies. The fossil grouping helps narrow the range of rock ages to those known to have supported all the creatures present in the assemblage.

To date fossils less than seventy thousand years old, paleontologists employ the radiometric carbon-14 process. For older fossils, stratigraphic position and noncarbon radiometry on surrounding rock are used. The oldest fossils found so far are prokaryotes, single-cell organisms without nuclei, exposed in Australian chert, a fine-grained silica rock 3.5 billion years old.

**PHASE TWO**
Sediments such as sand or mud pile on top of the remains before they rot, sedimenting them into place. The pressure of sediment from above turns the lower sediments into rock.

**PHASE THREE**
Mineral-laden water percolates through the rock, filling the space between the organism's cells. Sometimes the minerals replace the bones or shells.

**PHASE FOUR**
Millions of years later the rock is uplifted. Weathering and erosion expose the fossil to view.

# Reading Rock

Every rock has a story to tell. Hold one in your hand and you can sometimes read the evidence of its past yourself. Striations speak of passing glaciers; a surface worn smooth may reflect eons of relentless winds; pitting suggests battering by increasingly acidic rains. On a grander scale, when layered in strata, rocks relate not only their own tales, but also the stories of the prehistoric earthquakes, the fiery volcanic eruptions, and the ancient seas that sculpted the surrounding landscape.

*A stone outcropping on Point Lobos, California, reveals repeated beds of limestone and sandstone that have been tilted by plate action and then weathered smooth.*

*This rock tells a traveler's tale. Carried off by a glacier, it was abandoned in a new place when the ice withdrew; hence its name: glacial erratic.*

### DECIPHERING STRATA

Geologists read sedimentary sequences—the order in which the rock layers were laid down. Their interpretation depends on two key facts: Sedimentary rock is always laid down horizontally and if the rock layers have been undisturbed, the oldest rock will lie on the bottom. So it follows, for example, that if the rock layers are not horizontal, then the rock must have changed position over time. It also follows that the more bent and fractured and tilted the rock layers, the more change that has taken place—and, therefore, the older they are. Sometimes the layers are buckled over so far that, all these millions of years later, geologists have to figure out which way is up, an exercise in deduction called younging.

Another thing geologists know to be true—no matter where they are—is that if the same sequence is visible in rock outcrops in different places, it is likely that these beds are or once were continuous. Weathering and erosion may have removed the intervening rock.

### COAL-BEARING SEQUENCES

One sedimentary sequence frequently described by nineteenth-century British geologists includes repetitive layers or seams of coal. Such sequences were laid down during the Carboniferous Period (360 to

286 million years ago) when more plant materials were transformed into coal than in any other period. The depositions followed a pattern, always read from the bottom up: limestone, shale, siltstone, sandstone, underclay, and coal. After the coal, the progression repeats itself. Because the sequences often formed both in air and under seawater, the limestones and shales tend to be rife with marine fossils. These repetitive sequences are called cyclothems. In the United States, similar cyclothems have been described. Not all cyclothems have the complete set of beds, but each one of them has basically the same sequence.

*An illustration from a nineteenth-century British textbook shows a sedimentary sequence typical of what might be found in England.*

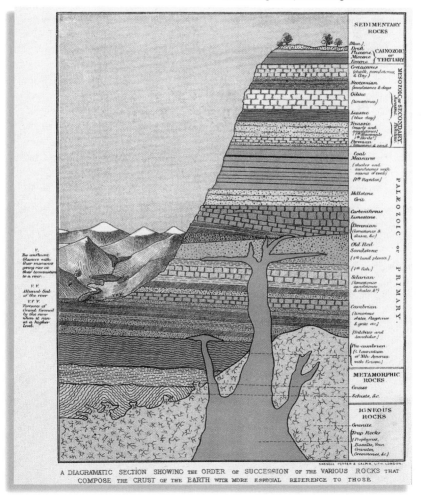

A DIAGRAMATIC SECTION SHOWING THE ORDER OF SUCCESSION OF THE VARIOUS ROCKS THAT COMPOSE THE CRUST OF THE EARTH WITH MORE ESPECIAL REFERENCE TO THOSE

# The Great Unconformity

**B**oth in the makeup and order of its strata, a sedimentary sequence is rich in clues about the geological history of an area. But sometimes what's missing from the rock record is as important as what is there. The sequence may contain a gap in time that geologists call an unconformity, a place where a young layer of rock lies directly on top of a much older layer of rock. The intervening "middle-aged" layers that you would expect to see are absent. The unconformity represents the boundary or contact between these two rock layers. The missing layers have been eroded away, and overlain a few million years later with fresh layers of sediment.

There are different kinds of unconformities. For example, a type known as a paraconformity marks a break in the sedimentary sequence where the fossil record, or faunal succession, is the only clue that something is missing. Easily seen with the naked eye is another type called an angular unconformity, where sediments rest on top of rock that has been deformed before being eroded. The most famous of these in North America is the Great Unconformity. It stretches from Arizona all the way into Alberta, Canada, and its history is not the same everywhere along its path.

Probably the best place to see the Great Unconformity is in the depths of the Grand Canyon. Hikers who make the trek some four thousand feet (1,220 m) into the canyon can actually touch places where tilting two-billion-year-old metamorphic rock contacts the horizontal layers of five-hundred million-year-old sedimentary rock—

*The Grand Canyon was probably created five million years ago, when the Colorado River cut through more than four thousand feet (1,220 m) of sedimentary rock. The swiftly moving waters eroded the surface of the rock, exposing the Great Unconformity between the Tapeats sandstone above and the Vishnu schist below.*

*Vishnu schist, the oldest rock in the Grand Canyon, is a metamorphic complex named after Vishnu's Temple, a rock formation on the Colorado River. Vishnu is a Hindu god.*

morphic rock, and the forces of weathering scoured and flattened its surface. For a time, a shallow sea covered it. As the water withdrew, it left behind tidal sediments such as sands and muds. A long period of subsidence and deposition followed, accompanied by remarkably little tilting, leaving the surface buried beneath more than four thousand feet (1,220 m) of sediment. The lowest layer of this sediment is called the Tapeats sandstone and the boundary between its bottom layer and the surface of the older Vishnu schist represents one area where the Great Unconformity has been exposed to view by the relentless erosion worked by the Colorado River.

thus spanning a 1.5-billion-year-old gap with their fingers. The ancient rock is called the Vishnu schist. It was sedimentary rock until about 1.7 billion years ago, when tectonic forces squeezed it into metamorphic rock, and pushed and shoved until the rocks tilted at an angle from their original horizontal position.

An igneous intrusion from the magma below penetrated this dark meta-

Photographed with polarized lights,
mica shows light-wave interference.

# MINERAL KINGDOM

# MINERAL MAKEUP

*The thousands of kinds of minerals in the rocks beneath our feet and in the collector's cabinet are all made from the same building blocks—chemical elements found in the Earth's crust.*

Holding a piece of rosy-colored granite in your hand, you can read the story of its makeup from its glittering components. The pink grains are feldspar, the white ones quartz, and the shiny black flecks mica. Each of these substances belongs to the kingdom of minerals. To a scientist, minerals all fit a precise definition. They are naturally occurring solid materials at room temperature, and they are non-organic in origin—that is, they were not produced by living organisms. So amber, for example, the fossilized sap from trees, and pearl, the creation of an oyster, are not considered minerals by the scientist, however much they may be valued by the collector.

Not all inorganic substances are minerals. Minerals must be very uniform inside, so that each piece of a mineral, even the smallest microscopic speck, is essentially the same. This uniformity can be traced to the regular repeating latticework of submicroscopic particles, called atoms, that makes up the mineral. This latticework also accounts for a mineral's distinctive chemical composition and it determines many of its properties.

## THE ELEMENTS

Everything on our planet is made up of chemical elements, from the oxygen in the air we breathe to the iron of a suspension bridge. There are ninety elements that

CHEMICAL SYMBOL

ATOMIC NUMBER

ELEMENT NAME

ELEMENTS OF MAJOR ABUNDANCE IN EARTH'S CRUST

| | | | | | | | | | | | |
|---|---|---|---|---|---|---|---|---|---|---|---|
| H 1 Hydrogen | | | | | | | | | | | |
| Li 3 Lithium | Be 4 Beryllium | | | | | | | | | | |
| Na 11 Sodium | Mg 12 Magnesium | | | | | | | | | | |
| K 19 Potassium | Ca 20 Calcium | Sc 21 Scandium | Ti 22 Titanium | V 23 Vanadium | Cr 24 Chromium | Mn 25 Manganese | Fe 26 Iron | Co 27 Cobalt | Ni 28 Nickel | Cu 29 Copper | Zn 30 Zinc |
| Rb 37 Rubidium | Sr 38 Strontium | Y 39 Yttrium | Zr 40 Zirconium | Nb 41 Nobelium | Mo 42 Molybdenum | Tc 43 Technetium | Ru 44 Ruthenium | Rh 45 Rhodium | Pd 46 Palladium | Ag 47 Silver | Cd 48 Cadmium |
| Cs 55 Cesium | Ba 56 Barium | La 57 Lanthanum | Hf 72 Hafnium | Ta 73 Tantalum | W 74 Tungsten | Re 75 Rhenium | Os 76 Osmium | Ir 77 Iridium | Pt 78 Platinum | Au 79 Gold | Hg 80 Mercury |
| Fr 87 Francium | Ra 88 Radium | Ac 89 Actinium | Rf 104 Rutherfordium | Ha 105 Hahnium | Sg 106 Seaborgium | Ns 107 Neilsborium | Hs 108 Hassium | Mt 109 Meitnerium | Uun 110 Ununilium | Uuu 111 Unununium | Uub 112 Ununbium |

| | | | | | | | | | |
|---|---|---|---|---|---|---|---|---|---|
| Ce 58 Cerium | Pr 59 Praseodymium | Nd 60 Neodymium | Pm 61 Promethium | Sm 62 Samarium | Eu 63 Europium | Gd 64 Gadolinium | Tb 65 Terbium | Dy 66 Dysprosium | Ho 67 Holmium |
| Th 90 Thorium | Pa 91 Protactinium | U 92 Uranium | Np 93 Neptunium | Pu 94 Plutonium | Am 95 Americium | Cm 96 Curium | Bk 97 Berkelium | Cf 98 Californium | Es 99 Einsteinium |

Mo 42 Molybdenum

Mg 12 Magnesium

occur naturally in the world around us and twenty-two more that have been created artificially in the lab. Just eight of them constitute almost all matter on earth. The two most common, oxygen and silicon, together account for about 73 percent of all matter by weight in the Earth's crust.

The characteristics of an element are based on the material's unimaginably small particles—its atoms. Atoms, in turn, consist of three types of even smaller particles: protons, neutrons, and electrons. Protons are positively charged particles and neutrons—as the name suggests—are neutral particles. Both protons and neutrons are found in the compact nucleus of the atom. Whizzing around the nucleus are the negatively charged electrons.

The number of protons in an element's nucleus is referred to as

> *"Circumstantial evidence can be overwhelming. We have never seen an atom, but we nevertheless know that it must exist."*
>
> — Isaac Asimov

its atomic number and determines what the element is. The number of protons and neutrons together is referred to as atomic mass. In the atom of any given element, the number of neutrons can vary, affecting the atomic mass. Atoms of the same element that have a different mass are called isotopes. Geologists use unstable isotopes in radiometric dating (*page 33*).

**BONDING**

Most elements do no usually exist as isolated atoms. By sharing or transferring electrons, atoms can bond with other atoms—of the same or of a different element. Minerals composed of just one kind of atom are pure elements, referred to as native elements: A piece of copper (Cu) is made up solely of copper atoms. Other minerals are chemical compounds. For instance,

|  |  |  |  |  | He 2<br>Helium |
|---|---|---|---|---|---|
| B 5<br>Boron | C 6<br>Carbon | N 7<br>Nitrogen | O 8<br>Oxygen | F 9<br>Fluorine | Ne 10<br>Neon |
| Al 13<br>Aluminum | Si 14<br>Silicon | P 15<br>Phosphorus | S 16<br>Sulfur | Cl 17<br>Chlorine | Ar 18<br>Argon |
| Ga 31<br>Gallium | Ge 32<br>Germanium | As 33<br>Arsenic | Se 34<br>Selenium | Br 35<br>Bromine | Kr 36<br>Krypton |
| In 49<br>Indium | Sn 50<br>Tin | Sb 51<br>Antimony | Te 52<br>Tellurium | I 53<br>Iodine | Xe 54<br>Xenon |
| Tl 81<br>Thallium | Pb 82<br>Lead | Bi 83<br>Bismuth | Po 84<br>Polonium | At 85<br>Astatine | Rn 86<br>Radon |
| 113 |  |  |  |  |  |

| Er 68<br>Erbium | Tm 69<br>Thulium | Yb 70<br>Ytterbium | Lu 71<br>Lutetium |
|---|---|---|---|
| Fm 100<br>Fermium | Md 101<br>Mendelevium | No 102<br>Nobelium | Lr 103<br>Lawrencium |

**The Periodic Table of Elements**

*Elements are typically presented in a chart based on the periodic repetition of certain chemical properties. Each element has a symbol based on its English or Latin name. They are ordered according to their atomic number, which is determined by the number of protons in the element's nucleus. For example, silicon (Si) contains fourteen protons in its nucleus, so its atomic number is 14. Highlighted elements are those most abundant in the Earth's crust. Originally established in a simpler form by Dmitri I. Mendeleev in 1869, the periodic table has been modified over the years to take into account the discovery of new elements and a deeper understanding of the relationship between elements.*

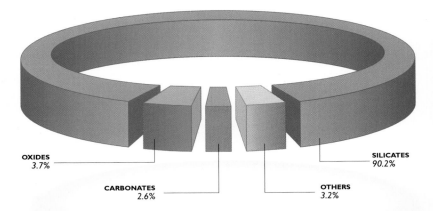

OXIDES
3.7%

CARBONATES
2.6%

SILICATES
90.2%

OTHERS
3.2%

**Mineral Families in the Earth's Crust**
Silicates make up almost all the minerals in the Earth's crust. Oxides and carbonates are the next most prevalent.
The remaining families constitute only a small piece of the pie.

the mineral stibnite is formed from atoms of antimony (Sb) and sulfur (S). The atoms bond to one another to form a regular repeating lattice. In that lattice, there are two atoms of antimony for every three of sulfur, so the formula for the compound is $Sb_2S_3$.

Atoms can bond in different ways, and the nature of these bonds affects some of the physical properties of the resulting substance, such as its hardness, its ability to conduct electricity, or its slipperiness. For example, the atoms in the mineral talc, $Mg_3Si_4O_{10}(OH)_2$, are tightly

bonded together into sheets, but the bonds between the sheets are very weak. Even the slightest force will cause the weak bonds to break and allow the sheets to slide apart. This gives talc its slippery feel and therefore its usefulness as a lubricant.

Many minerals, such as gold and quartz, have been known since the beginning of human time. Today, however, mineralogists recognize about thirty-five hundred mineral types, or species, and new ones are still being discovered. One recent discovery is moydite (Y), a few specimens of which were uncov-

## How to Read Mineral Formulas

Each mineral has a precise chemical makeup, which is expressed in a formula using the chemical symbols for each element. Most minerals occur as compounds consisting of two or more elements. Quartz, for example, has the formula $SiO_2$, indicating that it is made up of both silicon (Si) atoms and oxygen (O) atoms, in a ratio of one to two. Quartz is one of the relatively few minerals with constant composition. Any sample, from a tiny grain to a huge boulder, will contain these two elements in these proportions.

ered in the mid-1980s in the Evans-Lou Mine in Quebec.

## DANA SYSTEM

To make sense of the bewildering array of minerals, scientists organize species into families based on their chemical makeup. The Dana system, first published in 1848 by Yale professor of mineralogy James Dwight Dana, is based on twelve classes and, although there have been modifications to the system since it was devised, it continues to be used by both scientists and collectors alike. This system has been followed in the Identification Guide that begins on page 94.

The first class in the Dana system is composed of the so-called native elements such as gold (Au), platinum (Pt), and sulfur (S). These minerals are made up of a single pure element and they exist in relatively small quantities in nature. The most abundant mineral family is the silicates, a group of minerals made up of the elements silicon (Si) and oxygen (O) combined with other elements. The silicates include a wide variety of minerals because the silicate groups ($SiO_4$) can link to one another in a variety of ways.

While silicates make up almost all of the Earth's crust, two less common classes, sulfides and oxides, are among the most valuable

### A Rainbow of Colors

Many minerals owe their distinctive color to a particular element in their chemical makeup. The red-orange of vanadinite, for instance, is due to the presence of the element vanadium. Often, however, the color of a mineral is due to minute traces of a foreign element. For example, beryl ($Be_3Al_2Si_6O_{18}$) is typically yellow, but when impurities are added the color changes: Aquamarine contains iron, emerald contains traces of chromium and/or vanadium, and red beryl contains manganese. Since the impurities occur in such tiny quantities (parts per million), the colored versions of the mineral are considered varieties of beryl rather than separate minerals.

to us on a day-to-day basis. They are the source of metals used for everything from filigree jewelry to steel girders. Some metals can be mined directly from the ground, but most are "locked up" in chemical compounds with other elements, such as those in the sulfide and oxide classes. The resulting minerals, referred to as metal ores, must be smelted or refined to get at the useful metal. In sulfides, metals form compounds with sulfur (S). The sulphide galena (PbS), for example, contains lead. Oxides contain oxygen (O) combined with some other element, often a metal, as in the case of hematite ($Fe_2O_3$), an oxide of iron (Fe).

# Crystals

Almost no one is immune to the attraction of nature's perfect crystals, with their mirror-smooth faces and intriguing geometric shapes. The word "crystal" itself comes from the Greek word for ice—a derivation rooted in the ancient Greek belief that crystals were formed of water frozen so hard it would never melt. In fact, since any naturally occurring inorganic solid with a crystalline structure is considered to be a mineral, ice itself is technically a mineral, albeit a difficult one to preserve in a collection. Solid materials that do not have a crystalline structure, such as obsidian, are referred to as amorphous.

Mineral crystals are make up of millions of tiny building blocks, called unit cells. All unit cells of a particular mineral are identical: they are each made up of exactly the same number and type of atoms in exactly the same configuration. Not only is every unit cell in a particular crystal identical, but so is every unit cell in every crystal of that mineral. So, when a large cubic crystal of table salt—the mineral halite—is broken up into smaller pieces, each piece has the same cubic structure. Even the grains of salt are tiny perfect cubes.

## CRYSTAL SYSTEMS

As crystals grow, their unit cells stack together in a three-dimensional form. This means that only certain shapes of unit cells are possible. Scientists have determined that there are six basic shapes, each one defined by the relative lengths

**Crystal Systems**
The building blocks for the six crystal systems are defined by the relative lengths of their axes and the angles between those axes. Each crystal system exhibits certain types of crystal symmetry.

**ISOMETRIC (CUBIC)**
Three axes of the same length, all intersecting at 90°. Possible symmetries: Mirror symmetry; 2-fold, 3-fold, and 4-fold symmetry; and center-of-symmetry.

**TETRAGONAL**
Two axes of equal length and one longer or shorter axis, all intersecting at 90°. Possible symmetries: Mirror symmetry; 2-fold and 4-fold symmetry; and center-of-symmetry.

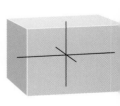

**ORTHORHOMBIC**
Three axes of different length, all intersecting at 90°. Possible symmetries: Mirror symmetry, 2-fold symmetry, and center-of-symmetry.

*Galena belongs to the isometric (cubic) system. Even though its basic building block is in the shape of a cube, it often exhibits other geometric faces. On this galena crystal (left), cubic faces are combined with octahedron (eight-sided) faces.*

of its axes and by the angles between its axes, and they have sorted minerals by these unit cell shapes into the six systems shown below.

You can visualize these axes as imaginary rods piercing the center of the crystal. A cubic crystal, such as that of halite or pyrite, has three axes of symmetry, all meeting at 90° and all of equal length. Other crystals, such as those of rutile, belong to the tetragonal system and have three axes of symmetry meeting at 90°, with one of them longer than the other, producing a brick-like shape.

The minerals belonging to each crystal system also exhibit certain distinctive types of symmetry, which can occasionally be seen

when the crystals have grown undistorted. To understand symmetry, hold up your hands with your fingers spread wide. Your hands are basically the same except that they are flipped as though one were the mirror image of the other. When opposite sides of a crystal are mir-

*Graphite and diamond are polymorphs: They have exactly the same chemical makeup, but owe their radically different properties to their different crystal structures.*

ror images of each other, the crystal is said to have mirror symmetry. If, when a crystal is rotated a half turn—180°—it looks the same as it did in its original position, then that crystal is said to have two-fold

**MONOCLINIC**
*Three axes of different length, one angle not 90°. Possible symmetries: Mirror plane symmetry, 2-fold symmetry, and center-of-symmetry.*

**TRICLINIC**
*Three axes of different lengths, all three angles of intersection are not 90°. Possible symmetry: Center-of-symmetry.*

**HEXAGONAL**
*Four axes: three axes of equal length and one longer or shorter axis; equal length axes intersect at 60°. Possible symmetries: Mirror plane symmetry; 2-fold, 3-fold, and 6-fold symmetry; and center-of-symmetry.*

symmetry. If when it is rotated a quarter turn—90°—it looks the same, then the crystal is said to exhibit four-fold symmetry. Crystals can also have three-fold symmetry, six-fold symmetry, and/or a center-of-symmetry, which means every one of its points has a corresponding identical point on the opposite side, the same distance from its center.

### CRYSTAL FORMATION

In a familiar experiment, a string is hung in a dish of hot water saturated with salt. As the water cools, the string becomes encased in a layer of glittering salt crystals. This is exactly how crystals form in nature. Cracks in rocks fill with liquid saturated with dissolved elements, and crystals precipitate on the rock faces. Crystals can also precipitate when a saturated solution begins to evaporate or when molten material cools.

Asbestos, the name for any of several minerals that can be separated into flexible fibers, has a fibrous habit. The longer fibers can be woven into fireproof cloth, shorter fibers are used in paper and a variety of building materials.

Many crystals form under conditions of incredible pressure and temperature. They can grow in a few days, as in the case of the crystals in the dish, or they can take millions of years to form within magma. The conditions under which crystals develop can affect both the kind of bonds formed at the atomic level and the arrangement of the atoms in crystals.

Sometimes the same elements form more than one kind of crystal structure—the minerals that result are called polymorphs. No two minerals could be as dissimilar as graphite and diamond. Yet both have the same chemical composition—pure carbon. The carbon atoms in graphite, used as the so-called lead in pencils, are held together in sheets with relatively weak bonds between them. The sheets easily slip apart, leaving a

### The Perfect Crystal

The search for the perfect crystal has been the Holy Grail of mineralogy. Even crystals grown in labs are distorted by gravity, the one force that can't be escaped, at least not on Earth. Establishment of permanent space stations has changed all that. In the zero gravity conditions of Mir, scientists have been able to grow near perfect crystals of a man-made mineral species, triglycine sulfate.

black mark on a piece of paper. In contrast, the atoms in a diamond are held together by a three-dimensional network of powerful atomic bonds, yielding a mineral that is used in blades to cut through steel.

Unfortunately for the collector, well-formed crystals, with smooth, evenly proportioned faces, are not common in nature. Growing in cracks in rocks, as they often do, crystals are hemmed in on all sides and their natural shape may be distorted. If crystals manage to grow much faster in one direction than another, they will end up thin and needlelike. If crystals grow too quickly, the faces will be distorted and small, and all that will be visible to the naked eye is a grainy surface.

## CRYSTAL HABIT

The general shapes of crystals or the way groups of crystals grow together in a mineral sample is referred to as that mineral's crystal habit—often used as an aid in its identification *(page 82)*. Terms such as reniform (rounded kidney-shaped masses) and bladed (looks like a knife blade) are used to describe mineral habit. Depending on the conditions in which it forms, the same mineral can adopt more than one habit. Quartz, for example, has a variety of habits. If the quartz grows crystals in long columns, its habit is known as prismatic. Quartz in nondescript chunks consisting of many tiny inter-grown crystals is referred to as having a massive habit. At the atomic level, however, all types of quartz have the same crystal structure.

*Twinning is a particularly spectacular crystal habit. The minerals that exhibit this habit can grow with one crystal piercing through the surface of another or with their crystals sharing faces, creating striking shapes—from a simple cross to the spokes of a wheel. Minerals that are frequently found twinned include cerussite, chrysoberyl (below), and rutile.*

## CRYSTAL CLEAVAGE

By the time crystals make it to the collector's cabinet, they are rarely in pristine condition. Typically samples have been chipped or split apart along flat planes, whether by a miner's hammer or by natural changes in temperature and pressure. Although the original crystal habit may be impossible to recognize in a damaged specimen, the particular way the crystal has broken or split—referred to as cleavage—can help with identification. Some minerals break apart along weak points in their crystal structure, and depending on that structure, a mineral may break in one, two, or more directions. Mica, for example, bonds in sheets and can be easily cleaved in flat layers (cleavage in one direction), while galena cleaves in three directions into cubes.

The smoothness of the cleaved faces, referred to as cleavage quality, can also be a clue to mineral identification. For example, when fluorite cleaves, it reveals very smooth surfaces, referred to as perfect cleavage. Zircon, on the other hand, reveals somewhat irregular surfaces and is referred to as having poor cleavage.

Cleavage should not be confused with hardness. Diamond is the hardest mineral known—meaning it is almost impossible to scratch—but it cleaves perfectly.

## CRYSTAL FRACTURE

Depending on how they are struck, some minerals will fracture instead of cleaving, breaking at random to leave rough surfaces and edges that don't define any kind of clear plane. Fractured surfaces can be completely uneven, or they can be smooth and curved like a shell—referred to as conchoidal. Some minerals will cleave when struck in one direction and fracture in another.

## OPTICAL PROPERTIES

An especially appealing quality of many minerals is the way they glint and sparkle. The manner in which a

*The transparent mineral calcite cleaves into perfect rhombohedra.*

mineral reflects and transmits light is connected to its crystal structure. One of the first things you notice when you look at a crystal is whether you can see through it, and this depends on how the light is bent by the crystal. If you can see an object through the mineral, it is considered to be transparent. If light passes through but an object is not discernable, the mineral is translucent. If light does not pass through the sample at all, the mineral is opaque. Some crystals bend light in

*Pyrite, otherwise known as fool's gold, has tricked many people with its shiny metallic luster.*

light much like a polished silver tray does and are said to have a metallic luster, while the soft glow of the surface of certain varieties of gypsum is referred to as pearly.

Minerals that phosphoresce, or glow in the dark, owe this to the fact that light is absorbed by imperfections in the crystal structure and later released.

special ways as the beam passes through. For example, an object placed behind a clear piece of calcite will appear to be doubled.

The particular quality and intensity of the light reflected by the surface of a crystal is referred to as luster. The type of luster depends on how much light is reflected by the crystal surface and how much is absorbed. Minerals such as gold and galena reflect

Some minerals, such as cordierite, exhibit a beautiful change of color as they are rotated in light. The colors are produced because of the differences in how light is absorbed when it passes through the crystal from several different directions.

## Pseudomorphs

Sixteenth-century artist Michelangelo painted the Sistine Chapel with brilliant blue paint made from a powder of the mineral azurite. Centuries later, the blue had turned to green. The change in color was a clue that the mineral in the paint had actually changed its identity. As it loses water, the chemical makeup of azurite is altered slightly and the crystal structure transformed to create the green mineral malachite. The process can be observed in samples such as the one shown above, which contains both minerals. Despite the chemical change, the outward shape of the mineral specimen remains unaltered. This kind of transformed mineral is referred to as a pseudomorph.

# EARTHLY TREASURES

*Rich mineral deposits are created deep in the Earth's crust by a variety of geologic processes and then brought to the surface through uplift and erosion, where humans can mine them.*

It is one of the world's great ironies that those minerals for which we have little economic use—such as the rock-forming silicates biotite and hornblende—tend to be found in far greater abundance in the Earth's crust than minerals that are prized. Aluminum, for example, although it is the most plentiful metal in the crust, makes up only 8 percent of the crust by weight. Iron makes up a mere 5.8 percent, and magnesium only 2 percent.

> *"Earth fills her lap with pleasures of her own: Yearnings she hath in her own natural kind."*
>
> — WILLIAM WORDSWORTH

Profitable extraction of a mineral from the Earth requires much higher concentrations than this. The mining of iron, for instance, calls for concentrations of about 50 percent. Fortunately, geologic processes have concentrated valuable minerals in deposits that make their mining worthwhile.

chamber. Some of the lighter components in the magma work their way into cracks in the surrounding rock and are often carried even farther by groundwater, eventually forming large bands of minerals referred to as hydrothermal veins. The minerals formed in this way are known as vein minerals. Some are compounds, mineral ores that are primarily sulfides, oxides, and silicates from which metals, such as lead, can be recovered. But a few vein minerals are native elements, including the metals gold, silver, and platinum, and nonmetals such as carbon and sulfur. Other deposits are formed when hot solutions of dissolved minerals spread into porous rock, forming disseminated deposits; much of the world's copper is extracted from such deposits.

## INSIDE THE EARTH

Heat from the mantle or generated by movements of the crust melts rocks, forming magma. The magma collects in chambers in the Earth's crust. As it cools and begins to resolidify, the heavier minerals within it settle to the bottom of the

## ON THE SURFACE

When rocks are thrust up to the surface of Earth, their mineral components continue to concentrate. Removing water is one of the surest ways to concentrate a mineral deposit. Water evaporated from ancient saline lakes, for example,

*Gold, one of our most valuable mineral resources, generally forms in quartz and sulfide veins. With weathering, the gold nuggets are freed and carried away by streams where they settle in placer deposits.*

leaves behind rich deposits of minerals such as gypsum, which we use for plaster, and halite, which we consume as table salt.

Weathering and erosion also produce residual deposits of valuable minerals: rivers and streams strip small particles of minerals from exposed rock and carry them away, depositing them in riverbeds and lakes where they can be retrieved.

Gem minerals as well as tin and gold are found in such so-called placer deposits, which sparked the gold-rush frenzy of the last century.

### FINITE RESOURCES

Since concentration is a requirement, the mineral deposits that can be economically mined are finite. And since we use up minerals much, much more quickly than geologic processes can form them, these mineral resources are effectively non-renewable. Without a steady supply of minerals to sustain them, world economies will founder.

# Mines & Mining

Whole eras of human history have been defined by the ability to mine and process minerals, particularly metals. By 4000 B.C., ancient peoples had already learned that through the heating of certain kinds of rocks, they could extract copper to make tools and weapons. By 3000 B.C., they were combining copper with tin to produce a harder metal, giving birth to what is known as the Bronze Age. Fifteen hundred years after that, humans had entered the Iron Age. Modern times have brought so many technological advances that no single name would suffice, but the ability to locate and extract minerals from the Earth continues to progress, both in scale and efficiency.

*An open-pit mine such as this Utah copper mine is rarely more than two thousand feet (610 m) deep. Such mines are excavated in layers, forming a series of rock ledges called benches.*

### FINDING MINERAL DEPOSITS

Until this century, locating mineral resources was a somewhat haphazard process. Guided by a knowledge of how minerals are often found in association with certain geological features, prospectors would scour the landscape hoping to stumble on valuable samples. Today scientists still read the landscape, but they often use quite sophisticated aerial and satellite photos. These photos reveal large-scale geological features that may suggest the presence of a valuable mineral. For example, kimberlite pipes—a certain type of rock formation that may contain diamonds—show themselves on such photos as round, light-colored areas.

*This South African gold miner is drilling blasting holes into the walls of a tunnel. Some gold mine tunnels are more than 3 miles (4.8 km) deep, with temperatures measuring as much as 140°F (60°C).*

Once the possible site of a valuable deposit is identified, tests must be performed to confirm the find. Electric currents can be sent into the rock to measure its electrical resistance. An instrument called a magnometer may be used to locate magnetic materials such as magnetite and ilmenite. Geiger counters are employed to test for radioactive minerals such as uranium and thorium. Soil and vegetation analysis may reveal traces of metals absorbed from below. And drilling for rock samples, which are tested in a lab to check what they contain, is still one of the most common testing methods.

Even with all these modern techniques, serendipity still often plays a role in mineral exploration. One alert geologist, for instance, discovered an important source of gold by noticing the squeak his boots made as he walked across a rocky surface in Nevada. The sound indicated the presence of quartz in the rocks—a mineral sometimes found in association with gold.

### EXTRACTING MINERALS

After a site's promise has been confirmed, the minerals are either skimmed off the surface or dug from within the ground. Surface mining techniques include strip mines, open-pit mines, and placer mines. Strip mining—used for extracting such minerals as bauxite (an ore of aluminum)—removes topsoil in lengthy swaths; the ore is then scooped up with heavy machinery. Coal, not strictly a mineral since it is organic, often is mined this way.

In open-pit mining, a huge excavation is cut into the ground to get at dispersed and low-grade deposits of minerals such as copper ores. The copper mines of Arizona and Utah can cover up to three square miles (8 sq km) and pro-

---

### Quarrying Stone

An age-old form of mining seeks a material that, unlike ore, needs no processing: rock itself. But quarrying can be heavy work. Building stones—typically granite, limestone, slate, and marble—are cut from surrounding rock in large blocks: A block of granite cut from a larger granitic mass may measure twenty feet (6 m) in height and weigh as much as two thousand tons—equivalent to forty loaded tractor trailers. The marble excavated in this quarry in the Italian Alps is the same as that used by Michelangelo. It is still a favorite material of sculptors today.

duce enough copper per year to wire millions of new homes.

A final type of surface mining mimics the gold panning of the last century. While nineteenth-century prospectors in the Klondike and California gold fields used small pans to sift through silt and pebbles from river beds, commercial dredging machines now scoop up huge shovelfuls of sand or gravel from placer deposits and sort through the material for gold nuggets or gemstones. A tin ore called cassiterite is also recovered this way. Dredgers working off the coast of Malaysia process up to sixteen thousand tons of cassiterite-rich gravel each day.

Reaching large veins of minerals such as lead, nickel, and zinc means digging deep underground mines. A typical mine may include mile-deep (1.6 km) shafts and a network of hundreds of miles of tunnels following the veins through the rock. The ore is blasted from the walls with explosives and transported in ore cars or conveyor belts to elevators that carry it to the surface. On the other hand, salt and sulfur, also located deep in the ground, can be extracted without a single miner having to go underground. Hot water, pumped into holes bored in the ground, dissolves the mineral. The resulting solution is then pumped up to the surface.

Whether a mineral deposit can be mined profitably depends on not only the kind of rock it is buried in but also such factors as labor costs, available technology, and the local transportation costs. For example, in Arizona, ore that contains only 0.5 percent copper is considered worth mining, while in Zambia, ore with concentrations of 4.4 percent copper is left in the ground. The cost of extraction and transport make the endeavor too expensive. Mines that were once profitable often shut down when the remaining ore is too deep to extract easily or when the mineral's market price changes.

## Biomining

In recent years, mining companies have begun to enlist the world's smallest miners—bacteria, such as thiobacillus ferooxidans, that can chew their way through metal ores. In a technique referred to as biomining, bacteria cause an oxidizing reaction in ore that releases the metal. This technique can extract gold from low-grade ores where other processing methods fail. Biomining is now standard practice for processing copper—about one-quarter of the world's copper is processed this way. Similar bacteria techniques are also being employed in cleanup operations to extract contaminants from soil polluted by mining operations.

### MINERAL PROCESSING

Once a metallic ore has been taken from the ground, it has to be processed to extract the metal it contains. This is often done right at the mine site. Huge smelting ovens melt down ore and separate metal from the waste, or gangue, which is then discarded.

*Different minerals can be a source of the same metal. Shown here are five iron ores: two kinds of hematite (far left), pyrite (center bottom), magnetite (center top), and limonite (near left).*

In some cases, metal can be extracted from an ore through a chemical process. In one method for processing gold ore, beds of the ore are sprayed with a cyanide solution that leaches out the metal; the gold-rich solution then is collected in large vats and passed through carbon filters to recover the gold.

Sometimes the byproducts of one type of mineral processing can yield another valuable material. Silver, for instance, is often extracted from the waste material produced by the processing of lead and copper. Waste sulfates yield sulfur, which is converted into sulfuric acid and used in a myriad of industrial applications.

### MINING AND THE ENVIRONMENT

Cutting massive swaths and craters in the Earth has serious deleterious effects on the environment. Surface mining robs the location of natural vegetation and leaves unsightly piles of waste rock. Drainage water from mineral processing carries off acids into nearby streams and lakes, damaging aquatic life. Underground mines sometimes collapse, leaving huge gullies.

There are, however, methods of extracting mineral resources in a more environmentally responsible way. Many mining companies now refill strip mines, cover them with topsoil, and replant with local vegetation; waste rock from open-pit mines is often leveled and the pits allowed to fill with water to create attractive reservoirs; and underground tunnels can be backfilled as work proceeds. Drainage water from processing can be chemically neutralized before it is released into natural waterways. Public awareness of the environmental impact of mining helps promote these kinds of solutions.

**Finding a Mineral in a Flash**
Some minerals are located by unlikely seeming techniques. For example, sphalerite, a major ore of zinc, has a special property known as triboluminescence: When sphalerite is rubbed or scratched, it glows. To locate a vein, miners run a metal pick across mine walls and watch for a telltale flash of light.

# Ocean Minerals

For decades now, efforts have been made to mine the oceans for their minerals. Both the ocean floor and the water above it hold a wide range of valuable elements. Indeed it has been estimated that as much as ten thousand million tons of gold may be dissolved in the oceans' water, although recent efforts to extract some of this wealth required the processing of fifteen tons of seawater in order to obtain 0.000003 ounces (0.09 mg) of the metal. More successful is the mining of alluvial diamond deposits in shallow water off the shore of South Africa.

### EXPLORING THE DEEP

Although almost three-quarters of our planet is covered by ocean, the ocean floor remains largely unexplored. Only about 2 percent of it has been mapped in any detail. In fact, more is known about the dark side of the moon than of the ocean floor. Until recently, direct reconnaissance at the ocean bottom has been limited—with diving suits, divers can survive trips to depths of two thousand feet

(610 m) or so, but quickly run out of air supply. Today, however, deep-diving submarines are being used to transport two or three people at a time to the ocean floor, and robotic vehicles are also providing a wealth of data.

### OCEAN HOT SPRINGS

In the late 1970s, scientists exploring the mid-ocean ridge off the coast of Ecuador made an extraordinary discovery: enormous black plumes shooting up from the ocean floor. Further investigation revealed that these plumes spouted from underground hot springs venting along the ridge. The springs were so hot, in fact, that they melted the temperature probe of the exploratory submarine. Scientists now know that as the tectonic plates that support the ocean floor spread apart, water slips down into the rift and is heated by the magma. The hot water reacts with many of the water soluble elements in the magma, and this fiery chemical soup spurts back up until it meets the near-freezing seawater above.

*A future source of minerals from the ocean's floor may be beds of these potato-sized manganese nodules. The nodules are found littering the ocean floor between South America and Hawaii. A profitable way to recover them has yet to be developed.*

*This hydrothermal vent off the coast of Mexico spews mineral-rich water at 650°F (343°C).*

springs. These creatures rely on chemicals in the water rather than sunlight for survival. Their survival in such conditions may provide a clue as to how life began in the oceans.

## MINING THE OCEAN FLOOR

About 140 sites of hydrothermal vents have been found around the globe. So far the interiors of only four have been sampled for their precise mineral content. Because of the huge expense, only a few drill holes have been made at each site, rather than the hundred or so that might be involving in sampling a site on land. The first site to be mined may be one in the Manus Basin off the shore of Papua New Guinea. An Australian mining company, in cooperation with the Papua New Guinean government, has already staked out 1,500 square miles (3,885 sq km) of the sea floor. However, the floor here is 5,000 feet (1,524 m) under water, and mining equipment that can operate at these depths has yet to be built.

Another challenge posed by these new mineral sources is that many sites are located in international waters. Agreements to ensure that the world's nations benefit equitably from the discoveries are required—not an easy undertaking.

Rapidly cooling, the solution releases its load of minerals, creating tall spires referred to as black smokers. Scientists believe that much of the water of the world's oceans is pumped through this giant circulation system—over a period of millions of years.

Exploration of the hot springs, or hydrothermal vents, has uncovered untold mineral wealth—zinc, copper, lead, silver, and gold—in deposits comparable to many land sites. And geologists and mining companies aren't the only ones delighted with the discovery of the vents. Biologists are thrilled with the giant worms, crabs, and clams they have found lurking around the

# A Multitude of Uses

Many of society's technological achievements have been based on ingenious exploitation of Earth's minerals—applications that range from using platinum for electrical connections to making lasers with corundum ruby. In ways both exotic and mundane, modern civilization is a mineral-based creation.

### HOUSEHOLD ITEMS

The houses we live in are constructed with a surprising number of mineral products. Wallboard contains gypsum; the mortar between the bricks contains sand that is typically grains of quartz; and some house paints contain mica. Copper, the first metal to be used extensively by humans, is today one of the most common minerals in our homes.

This is due in part to copper's ability to conduct electricity and in part to the fact that the material is easily rolled. About 195 pounds (88 kg) of copper goes into making the wiring hidden in the walls of a typical house, and another 151 pounds (68 kg) of copper account for the house's plumbing pipes and fittings. This native element is such an excellent material for piping that some five-thousand-year-old copper tubing, recently unearthed in Egypt, is still in usable condition.

Other native elements, such as gold and silver, have been treasured

*One of the mineral ingredients used to make fireworks is antimony, which occurs in nature both as a native element and also in sulfides, especially stibnite.*

by humans since the very beginning of recorded history. In fact, the approximately hundred thousand tons of gold that has been extracted from Earth so far is mostly still in use—although it is likely to have changed form countless times. The gold in a jewelry-store necklace, for instance, may once have been an ancient Roman coin.

### QUARTZ WATCHES

One of the most striking uses of a mineral is in the operation of wrist-watches. Crystals of quartz, one of the planet's most common minerals, have the unusual property of vibrating when an electric current passes through them. Eslectricity supplied by a watch battery sets the crystal vibrating about a hundred thousand times per second, which in turn precisely controls electrical pulses, causing the hands of the watch to move. The vibration is so regular that the crystal misses no more than a single vibration out of every ten billion.

Not only do we use minerals to construct and make things run, we also consume them. Iron, copper, and zinc are considered essential components of a healthy diet. We season our food with halite, better known as salt, and whiten our coffee with artificial creamers containing clay minerals. We patch our teeth with gold and platinum, and clean them with toothpaste, which contains silica (from quartz) as an abrasive, titanium oxide as a whitener, and fluoride (derived from the mineral fluorite) to pre-

## Silicon Chips

The complex circuitry of a home computer is etched onto thumbnail-sized chips of silicon. This element is the material of choice because it is an excellent semiconductor: Although it does not conduct electricity under normal conditions, it can be forced to conduct in a specific direction through

the addition of minute impurities. To manufacture silicon chips, crystals of pure silicon are grown in the lab and sliced into thin wafers—like those shown above—that are each about three to six inches (8 to 15 cm) in diameter. Once the circuitry has been added, the wafer is cut into a hundred or so individual chips, each containing millions of electrical connections.

vent decay. And in one delightfully extravagant use of a mineral, sweets made in India are often covered with a very thin leaf of silver.

# Gemstones

Since the beginning of human history, people have coveted beautiful and colorful stones, fashioning them into jewelry and other decorative objects. More than seven thousand years ago, Egyptians were stringing necklaces of turquoise beads; four thousand years ago the Chinese were working exquisite carvings of jade. The ancient peoples of Mexico and Central America even set small bits of turquoise into their teeth. Our ancestors so revered gemstones that they often credited them with magical properties. In the Middle Ages, for instance, a pendant of aquamarine was believed to invest its wearer with foresight. Roman women believed that an amethyst would ensure faith-

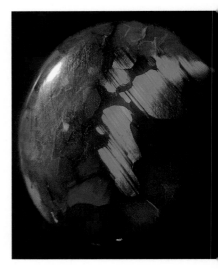

fulness by their husbands. Today, however, the value of a gemstone resides primarily in three properties: beauty, rarity, and durability.

The most valuable gemstones—diamonds, rubies, emeralds, sapphires—were once commonly known as "precious" stones. They are brilliant, transparent, extremely hard, and exceptionally rare. Other gemstones, such as amethyst, garnet, and turquoise, are less rare and are traditionally referred to as "semiprecious." Often just as beautiful as the more highly prized stones, such gems are frequently priced within the reach of a collector.

### THE BEAUTY OF GEMSTONES

Gemstones are among the most brightly colored objects in nature—the blood red of a ruby or sea blue of a sapphire rivals the most brilliant blossom. The Burmese once believed that rubies ripened like fruit and that deep red stones were

---

## Flawed Beauties

Even the most valuable gem hides within it tiny flaws formed by bubbles of gas and minute crystal traces of other materials. These flaws, referred to as inclusions can often be seen only under a microscope. In some cases, inclusions reduce the value of a gem, but in others they are responsible for prized visual effects, such as the star in a star sapphire or the cat's eye in a chrysoberyl.

The study of inclusions has gained new importance with the advent of synthetic gems. Since these creations of the lab are often literally flawless, the presence of a tiny fleck or bubble is sometimes the only indication that the gem was formed in nature.

*The most valuable opals are black with a beautiful play of colors. Arab peoples believed that opals were formed in lightning bolts, acquiring their bright colors and then falling to Earth.*

the most fully ripe. The ancient Persians believed that the world was supported by an enormous sapphire, the color of which was reflected in the sky.

Many gemstones occur in a range of colors, depending on the presence of trace elements in their crystal structure. Peridot can be found in shades ranging from light yellow-green to dark olive. Some stones are even known by different names depending on their color. Sapphires and rubies, for example, are both varieties of the mineral corundum. Amethyst, a purple variety of quartz, can actually be transformed into its yellow sister, citrine, by heating; most of the citrines on the market are created in this way.

Diamonds, the most valuable precious stone, are highly prized when they are clear and colorless. However, a perfect diamond hides a rainbow of colors deep within it, flashing one or another as the light hits the

stone. This is due to a process known as dispersion. As a beam of light enters the gem, it is slowed down and split into its different wavelengths, spreading out into a full spectrum of colors. In some gems, the way the light is absorbed by the crystal depends on the direction from which the light comes. These gems display different colors as they are turned, a phenomenon that is referred to as pleochroism.

Two optical properties account for the brilliance of cut gemstones: reflectance, the way light bounces off the gem surface, and refraction, the way light is bent by the gem's crystal structure. The refractive index of a particular gem can be measured and is used by experts for identification. Gemologists choose the cut that creates facets to best enhance both of these properties.

*Crowns have historically been the showpieces of the world's rarest gems. The British Imperial State Crown, shown at right, is home to Saint Edward's Sapphire.*

*This uncut aquamarine is a variety of beryl, a mineral found primarily in Brazil.*

with beryls, topaz, and tourmaline. Gemstones are often carried from their original source as rock erodes and, because they are relatively heavy, they tend to settle out in gravel beds.

The first gemstones picked up by ancient peoples were probably found lying on beaches or stream beds, such as the gravel deposits of diamonds, sapphires, and rubies in India, Sri Lanka, and Burma. The oldest mines in the world are believed to be the lapis lazuli mines in Afghanistan. A source of gems known to Egyptian traders six thousand years ago, they still supply the world with high-quality stones. Today, gemstones are mined around the world, from South Africa to Brazil to Australia.

Because gemstones exist in the Earth's crust in such tiny quantities,

Many gemstones, such as turquoise and jade, are translucent or opaque and do not have the brilliance of a transparent gem. Their beauty resides in their lovely colors and in their softly glowing luster.

### THE ORIGIN OF GEMSTONES

Many gemstones are forged in a fiery cauldron deep within the Earth. Diamonds, for example, form 130 miles (200 km) or so below the surface at temperatures of up to 2,192°F (1,200°C) and are then thrust to the surface in pipes of kimberlite rock. Other gems crystallize in igneous and metamorphic rocks closer to the surface. Special deposits of igneous rock called pegmatites, for example, sometimes contain cavities studded

### Gemstones as Medicine

The mysterious powers ascribed to gemstones have prompted people to offer them as a cure for ailments. Often there was an association between the color of the ground stone and its perceived curative properties. Red stones, for instance, were believed to cure hemorrhages and calm anger, yellow stones were used to treat jaundice, and amethyst offered protection from drunkenness.

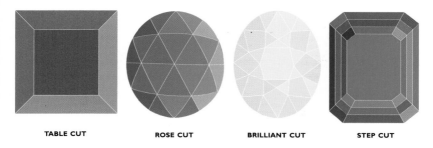

TABLE CUT          ROSE CUT          BRILLIANT CUT          STEP CUT

**Popular Gem Cuts**
*The art of faceting gemstones has a long history, and each style of cut has its own name. The oldest cuts, such as the table and rose cuts, date from Medieval Europe. More modern cuts include the brilliant and step cuts.*

they are extremely expensive to extract. Diamond miners, for example, must process a ton of kimberlite on average to get one carat of diamonds, only 20 percent of which are of gem quality. Because of its extreme hardness, non-gem quality stones are used as abrasives, saw blades, and drill bits.

Gemstones of one special class are not actually minerals at all—their origin is in plant and animal materials. Jet, a glowing black stone, is highly compressed coal; amber is fossilized tree resin *(page 38)*; pearls are formed from secretions within the shells of oysters; corals are the skeletons of tiny sea animals; and ivory is cut from the tusks of elephants and other mammals, including walruses and narwhals.

But scientists have learned how to manufacture versions of some of nature's most stunning products. Gemstones can now be created in the lab. Laboratory-grown rubies so perfectly match natural ones in all their physical properties that even experts sometimes have difficulty telling the two apart. About 80 per-

cent of the diamonds on the market today are in fact diamond look-alikes, a synthetic compound called cubic zirconia. Although most are destined for industry, some do find their place in rings and pendants.

**THE LAPIDARY'S ART**
Once a natural gemstone is cut and polished, it is referred to as a gem. A skilled gem-cutter, or lapidary, can transform an ordinary-looking pebble into a priceless jewel. To do this, the craftsperson must decide how to cut and polish the stone to show its beauty to best advantage. In the case of opaque or translucent stones such as opal or turquoise, this may mean polishing to a smooth dome, referred to as a cabochon. In the case of transparent precious stones, the lapidary usually cuts the piece in a series of mirrorlike facets. A properly cut diamond will take light in through its upper facets and completely reflect the light off of its rear facets and back through the upper facets to the viewer. The cutting and polishing of such a gemstone can take several months to complete.

# Legendary Gems

Certain gems are fantastic enough to warrant their own place in history. Sometimes their fame is linked to their age. Saint Edward's Sapphire, for instance, is set in the British Imperial State Crown and was reputedly worn by Edward the Confessor in 1042. The renowned Koh-i-noor, a 109-carat diamond mined in India, is almost seven hundred years old. Sometimes size can be a contributing factor to notoriety, as in the case of the very large stone given to Edward the Black Prince in 1367. The Black Prince Ruby is, in fact, not a ruby at all, but another oxide mineral called

spinel. Often a gem's fame can be traced to the exorbitant price it fetches at auction. One gem, the 100.10-carat pear-shaped "D" flawless diamond, was sold for $16.55 million in 1995—the highest price ever paid for a single diamond. But ultimately it is gemstones' one-of-a-kind beauty that sets them apart. One of the most famous beauties is the spectacular Cullinan diamond, discovered by

**Spectacular Sapphire**
*This sapphire, called a Padparadscha Sapphire, weighs 100 carats and is the largest known sapphire of this color. Discovered in Sri Lanka, it now draws sapphire afficionados from around the world to the gem hall at the American Museum of Natural History.*

**Hope Diamond**
*This infamous blue stone, worn by Louis XIV, once weighed 112 carats. Stolen in 1792 during the French Revolution, the stone resurfaced in Paris in 1825 at its present size of 45.5 carats. In 1830 it was purchased by London banker Thomas Hope, after whom it was named. Its other owners include an actress who was shot onstage while wearing it and a Russian prince who was stabbed to death by revolutionary assassins.*

Thomas Cullinan in 1905 in the Premier Mine in South Africa. In its rough form, the diamond weighed 3,106 carats, the largest single diamond ever found. It was subsequently cut to produce nine principal stones. The largest of these priceless pieces, the Great Star of Africa, weighs in at 530.2 carats and is set in the British Royal Scepter.

### Patricia Emerald
*The 632-carat Patricia Emerald was found in the Chivor mine in Colombia in the 1920s. Ironically, the blast that discovered this gem destroyed a much larger emerald of equal quality and color. The Patrica is on display at the American Museum of Natural History in New York.*

QUARTZ - ROCK CRYSTAL
QUARTZ - CRISTAL DE ROCHE
HOT SPRINGS, ARKANSAS

QUARTZ
BRISTOL, SOMERSET, ENGLAND
SHIRLEY COLLECTION

OPAL
WATERVILLE, DOUGLAS CO., WASHINGTON

OPAL, GEODE-HYALITE
OPALE, GEODE-HYALITE

# COLLECTORS' WISDOM

QUARTZ – AMETHYST
QUARTZ – AMETHYSTE

QUARTZ – ROCK CRYSTAL
QUARTZ – CRISTAL DE ROCHE
BOURG D'OISANS, DAUPHINE, FRANCE

QUARTZ – AMETHYST
QUARTZ – AMÉTHYSTE

# THE ART OF COLLECTING

*Whether a collection consists of tiny, perfect crystals,
ores from a single mine, or puzzling pseudomorphs, it testifies
to the fascination of the raw materials of nature.*

Great museum collections owe their richness to individual passion. The outstanding mineral collection of the Smithsonian Institution, for example, received its original impetus from Washington A. Roebling, builder of the Brooklyn Bridge. Roebling set out to collect a specimen of every known mineral, and by the time he died he had almost reached his goal. Most collectors are far less ambitious, but even on a limited budget they often find ways of accumulating large numbers of specimens that reflect their particular interests.

> *"But there is one single moment that is never quite duplicated...when the first specimen is secured."*
>
> — CHARLES WILLIAM BEEBE

### GETTING STARTED

Collectors relish the excitement of filling out their trove, but sometimes admit that nothing quite lives up to the heady early days when they first began collecting. Many rock and mineral collectors begin with a love of the outdoors. A walk along a country road or along the seashore offers plenty of opportunities for gaining familiarity with some of the most common types of rocks. Knowledge can be gleaned in town as well since building stone is most often taken from nearby quarries.

Many museums carry rock and mineral displays and have special exhibits on regional geology. Small starter kits, often available through museum gift shops, at nature stores, and by catalog, take you one step closer to collecting. The kit usually includes a cataloging tray along with a variety of specimens.

Rock and gem shows provide inspiration to beginners as well as a site for collectors to buy and exchange specimens. Among the better known in North America are the Gem and Mineral Society Show in Tucson, Arizona, in February, the East Coast Gem, Mineral, and Fossil Show in Springfield, Massachusetts, in August and the gathering of thousands of independent dealers at Quartzite, Arizona each January and February. Two of Europe's biggest shows are the Mineralientage München, held in Munich in October and the show in Ste. Marie-aux-Mines, France, held each spring.

Perhaps the best way to learn about collecting is to visit a local club. There you will meet people who share your budding interest and who can offer advice on how to proceed. Many

Micromounters require 10-power magnifying lenses or microscopes to admire the crystals that make up their collections.

clubs offer workshops on subjects such as cleaning and organizing specimens and understanding rock formations and crystal structures.

First collections often include a bit of everything, from a piece of granite picked up by the roadside to an eye-catching cube of shiny pyrite from a rock and gem show. In time, though, most collectors specialize. Some collect rocks rather than minerals, attracted to their solid shapes, rough textures, and interesting patterns. Most collect minerals, often concentrating on a single species in all its forms and varieties. There are collectors who try to acquire samples of all the species of minerals that occur in a particular geological environment and collectors drawn to the ores of a particular metal. Other specialties include gem minerals, fluorescent minerals, and polished slabs that show naturally formed patterns resembling animals or landscapes. For some collectors, the only criterion is that their crystals be beautiful.

Some enthusiasts seek to capture the nature of a mineral by collecting a particular set of incarnations. For instance, a collection could include a sample of the mineral in the rough; a sample of the mineral's crystals growing in an unusual habit; a single, well-formed crystal; and an ornament made from the mineral.

An increasingly popular collecting specialty focuses on micromounts—tiny clusters of mineral crystals, often less than 0.125 inch (0.3 cm) in size, that can be seen clearly only under a microscope. While large crystals are frequently distorted or damaged, micromount samples more often show perfect, exquisitely formed crystals. Microsamples are usually less expensive and easier to come by than larger specimens. Moreover, an entire collection can be conveniently stashed in simple cubed boxes or even egg cartons.

# Rock Hunting

When you purchase samples at a show, you know exactly what you're getting. A rock-hunting field trip, though, is always full of surprises.

Plan your first field trips with experienced rock hounds and take the time to learn from them. Rock and mineral clubs, museums, and universities organize field trips on a regular basis, and such outings will help you familiarize yourself with rock hunting techniques and equipment—from geological maps to hammers and digging implements.

### WHERE TO LOOK

A field trip can take you to sites just down the road or on the other side of the globe. Some rock hunting sites *(page 176)* are particularly famous: the Red Cloud Mine near Yuma, Arizona, for instance, is renowned for its red crystals of wulfenite. But almost any rocky area is a potential collecting site. Make sure you first have the per-

*Examining a specimen up close calls for a 10-power magnifying glass, available at nature stores and through geological supply catalogs.*

mission of the owner before collecting on private land. And always respect the "No Collecting" signs on public land.

Road and rail cuts reveal a lot about local geology *(page 91)*. Exposed seashore cliffs or river banks are also good choices, but don't chip at these natural rock faces. Instead, restrict your collecting to loose rocks at the base—and watch out for falling rocks.

Areas of ancient volcanic activity may be a common source of geodes *(page 26)* and many of the sites are open to the public. Working mines and quarries are generally off-limits. Rock dumps near abandoned mines may be accessible, but they are a dwindling source: Mining companies are starting to backfill mines and replant.

---

### Safety Tips

• Never enter an abandoned underground mine—collapsing walls are common.

• Wear a hard hat when hunting below a rock face.

• Always carry a compass and a good map.

• Wear sturdy gloves to protect your hands and steel-toed boots to protect your feet.

• Never throw rocks over the edge—there may be someone below.

---

## A ROCK HOUND'S TOOLS

Taking a sample may be as simple as picking up a specimen from the ground or as complicated as trying to dislodge a crystal unharmed from a piece of rock. The tools most commonly used include the following:

• Digging tools such as small trowels are needed to excavate clays. Small collapsible shovels and rakes come in handy when hunting through stream beds or mine dumps.

• Hammers include crack hammers for breaking apart rocks and various types of geologist's hammers for knocking specimens free. These should be used sparingly.

• Pry bars and rock-splitter chisels serve to enlarge a crack in a rock.

• Panning tools for gold or gems include a pan and a wire sieve.

• Penknives help to clear soil from the surface of specimens.

## KEEPING TRACK

Once you have extracted a sample, label it, recording the location and kind of rock in which the sample was found. You may want to add a rough sketch of the surrounding rock; or, you can photograph the location of each specimen, noting the film frame that corresponds to the site. Wrap large samples in tissue, newspaper or bubble wrap. Egg cartons and metal tins are handy for smaller samples.

Out of respect for other collectors, never take more than what you need for your collection, and don't leave behind specimens from other locations. Limit your impact on the surrounding rock and vegetation, and backfill any holes you've made.

*A chisel-head hammer is usually used for collecting sedimentary rock.*

*Geological maps indicate rock types and distribution on a topographical background. They are essential for exploratory field trips.*

# Cleaning & Cataloging

A rock or mineral collection affords maximum pleasure if the samples have been carefully cleaned and are well organized.

Thorough cleaning can uncover beauty in an ordinary-looking sample. To separate a crystal specimen from surrounding rock, you may need to chip it free gently with a hammer and chisel. A non-water-soluble mineral can be cleaned with a toothbrush under running water. A soft brush and distilled water are best for removing dirt from delicate crystals. For fine cleaning, experienced collectors employ a variety of tools, including tweezers, dental picks, and fine artists' brushes. Cotton swabs, a dust blower with a rubber bulb, or a can of compressed air will remove dust. Don't use it on delicate crystals, though.

### USING ACIDS FOR CLEANING

In some cases, acids can be used to remove unwanted material from the surface of a crystal. Hydrochloric acid dissolves limestone and carbonate minerals; oxalic acid eliminates iron stains; and acetic or hydrochloric acid removes calcite from the surface of other minerals.

Protect your eyes with goggles and wear gloves when working with acid. To prepare a cleaning solution, mix one part acid to ten parts water—always adding acid to the water, never the reverse. Test the solution first on an inconspicuous part of the specimen to be sure the solution won't cause damage as it removes waste material. After the solution has dissolved the unwanted material, wash the specimen in water along with a little ammonia to neutralize any remaining acid.

### CATALOGING A COLLECTION

A cataloging system allows you to organize your samples in a logical manner and record important information about each piece. How you set up your cataloging system depends on what features of the collection are of most interest to you. Collectors frequently group their minerals according to chemical composition, using a system such as the Dana

*Samples of aurichalcite have been simply but neatly and effectively organized in egg cartons and a box lined with tissues.*

At left is a showcase display of wulfenite specimens, all of which were gathered from the Red Cloud Mine in Arizona.

letters with a number to specify the order within the category.

Label each specimen. For large samples, apply a dab of white water-soluble paint to an inconspicuous spot and mark the code on it with a fine felt pen. Cover the mark with clear nail polish to keep it from smudging. For tiny samples, mark the code on the container itself.

Information corresponding to each catalog number can be kept in a notebook or a computer database. Note when and where each specimen was found and in what geological formation. For purchased samples, note the seller, the purchase price, and the date of purchase.

system (a modified version of which is used in the guide section of this book). They typically group rocks according to whether they are igneous, sedimentary, or metamorphic. But you can organize samples by many other methods, such as where they were found, their color, or their crystal system. Even an alphabetical system can be useful. The important thing is to choose one approach and stick to it.

Every time you acquire a new sample, assign it a catalog code. For example, you can begin each code with a series of letters that indicate the mineral category—such as SIL for silicate—and then follow the

Many serious collectors put their most prized samples on display in a glass-front cabinet, often mounting each specimen on a decorative base and adding attractive lighting. The bulk of most collections, however, goes into divided containers, such as drawers, beer flats or egg cartons. The latter containers can be stored in shallow drawers or cardboard boxes. For advice on what best suits your collection, consult your local rock and mineral club or nature store.

# Identifying Minerals

Amateur collectors can learn to identify many minerals by studying their appearance and applying a few simple tests to determine underlying properties. All of the traits used to identify a mineral arise from its chemical makeup *(page 46)* and crystal structure *(page 50)*. They include luster, transparency, color, streak, hardness, habit, cleavage, and specific gravity. Checking for all of these—except specific gravity—can be carried out in the field. The mineral identification flowchart on pages 86 to 87 provides guidelines for identifying some common minerals, using a selection of the characteristics contained in the following checklist of items.

**LUSTER AND TRANSPARENCY**

One of the first things an experienced collector may do to identify a mineral is hold it up and examine the way its surface reflects light, a property referred to as luster *(page 54)*. Metallic minerals such as enargite, which contains copper, and ilmenite, which contains iron, look and shine like metals. Minerals such as aragonite and mimetite, however, are nonmetallic-looking. Their luster is variously described as glassy, waxy, adamantine (diamond-like), pearly, resinous, or dull. A few minerals, including manganite and arsenic, appear somewhere in between in luster and are described as submetallic.

Whether light can penetrate a mineral determines its transparency and this too can aid in its identification. For instance, calcite is often transparent while cassiterite is translucent. Many minerals lie in the middle range—for example, fluorite is described as transparent to translucent. All metals are opaque.

**COLOR AND STREAK**

The color of a mineral may be a clue to its identity: Azurite is a distinctive blue, malachite a marbly green, and sulfur a powdery yellow. But some minerals come in several colors. Augite can be green, black, brownish, or even almost colorless.

*A mineral's streak is unique. Shown here are the streaks of four minerals (clockwise from far left): sphalerite, graphite, pyrite, and hematite.*

## MOHS HARDNESS SCALE

| | MINERAL | TESTING DEVICE |
|---|---|---|
| 1 | Talc | fingertip |
| 2 | Gypsum | fingernail |
| 3 | Calcite | penny |
| 4 | Fluorite | penknife |
| 5 | Apatite | penknife |
| 6 | Orthoclase | steel file |
| 7 | Quartz | n/a |
| 8 | Topaz | n/a |
| 9 | Corundum | n/a |
| 10 | Diamond | n/a |

*This ranking of ten common minerals (from softest to hardest) was developed by German mineralogist Friedrich Mohs in 1812. It is based on the rule that any mineral can scratch another mineral softer than itself. If no other minerals are at hand, a sample can often be tested by the common items listed at right.*

leave streaks from red to black. Most nonmetallic minerals leave white streaks.

### HARDNESS

A mineral's hardness refers to how difficult it is to scratch its surface—not how difficult it is to break it. The Mohs hardness scale *(chart at left)* arranges ten common minerals on a scale from softest to hardest. Each mineral in the list can scratch the ones before it and be scratched by the ones after it. Scratch test kits are available at nature shops and through supply catalogs. Each kit contains test samples of the ten minerals. To test the hardness of an unidentified mineral, try scratching its surface with each of the samples. (If the unidentified sample can be scratched by calcite but not by fluorite, for example, its hardness lies between 3 and 4.) After scratching the surface of your mineral, wipe away the dust and check carefully for

Fortunately, there is a way to limit the confusion. All samples of a given mineral usually have the same streak—the powder mark of a mineral. (Augite's streak is gray-green regardless of the sample's color.)

To test for streak, run a sample across an unglazed ceramic surface and examine the color left behind. Special tile streak plates are available at nature shops, but you can also use the back of a wall tile or the unglazed bottom of a bowl or vase. Minerals that are harder than the porcelain can't be tested in this way because the tile, rather than the sample, will powder.

Streak is also useful for distinguishing among metallic minerals. Metallic minerals

### Crystal Forms

*Individual mineral crystals grow in a variety of geometric forms that are organized into systems. Gold belongs to the cubic system. However, its crystals can also take the form of octahedrons and dodecahedrons, variations on the basic cube.*

**CUBE**

**DODECAHEDRON**

**OCTAHEDRON**

**Mineral Habits**
*Some common crystal habits are shown here with an example of a mineral that exhibits the habit. Each is named for objects that they resemble, such as needles, plates, or globes.*

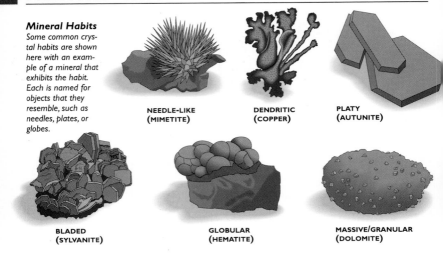

NEEDLE-LIKE
(MIMETITE)

DENDRITIC
(COPPER)

PLATY
(AUTUNITE)

BLADED
(SYLVANITE)

GLOBULAR
(HEMATITE)

MASSIVE/GRANULAR
(DOLOMITE)

a mark—the dust may come from either the test sample or the mineral being tested. If you see a scratch on the unidentified mineral, the test sample is harder. If you don't see a scratch, the unidentified mineral is harder or the two minerals have the same hardness. Examine the surface of the unidentified mineral with a magnifying glass to be sure. Instead of using the test samples to scratch the mineral you wish to identify, you can also use common objects that are equivalent to them in hardness such as a fingernail, a penny, a penknife, or a steel file.

**CRYSTAL FORM**
In cases where well-defined unbroken crystals are visible, the shape of the individual crystals can help identify the sample. The crystals of a single mineral species may appear in a variety of geometric shapes, referred to as their crystal forms. Forms are variations of the basic crystal system to which the mineral belongs *(page 50)*. In many cases, a mineral appears primarily in one or two of these forms: For example, fluorite samples typically grow as cubic crystals while calcite samples usually grow as rhombic crystals.

**MINERAL HABIT**
Sometimes confused with crystal form (described above), a mineral's habit is the way groups of its crystals tend to grow together, creating a distinctive overall form and texture. Experienced collectors can recognize the most common habits, shown above and opposite. While many minerals can appear in a variety of habits, some have only one or two, which can be an aid in identification. Sylvanite, for example, is most often bladed, copper is dendritic, and tourmaline is prismatic.

**CLEAVAGE AND FRACTURE**
Cleavage, the tendency of a mineral to break along characteristic planes, can also contribute to its identifica-

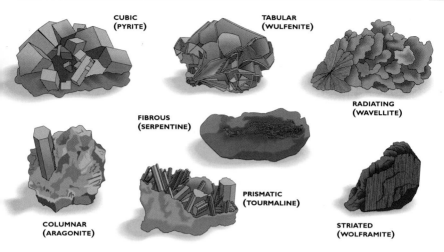

**CUBIC
(PYRITE)**

**TABULAR
(WULFENITE)**

**RADIATING
(WAVELLITE)**

**FIBROUS
(SERPENTINE)**

**PRISMATIC
(TOURMALINE)**

**COLUMNAR
(ARAGONITE)**

**STRIATED
(WOLFRAMITE)**

tion. Most minerals typically cleave in a certain number of directions. Muscovite, for example, cleaves in one direction, forming layers; fluorite cleaves in four directions, forming octahedrons.

Some minerals cleave cleanly into smooth planes, but the smoothness of the planes varies from species to species. The quality of cleavage is described as perfect, good, distinct, poor, or absent—

quartz, for example, doesn't cleave at all. Sometimes a mineral cleaves one way in one direction, but differently in the other or others: For example, scheelite has distinct cleavage in one direction and poor cleavage in two other directions.

If a mineral is broken in a direction that doesn't follow cleavage planes, it will fracture instead *(page 54)*. The quality of this fracture is characterized as uneven,

### Cleavage

*The shape of a broken sample is determined by the number of directions in which that mineral cleaves. Shown here are three typical cleavages in one, two, or three directions. Minerals with more than three cleavage planes can cleave into more complex shapes, such as the octahedrons formed by fluorite.*

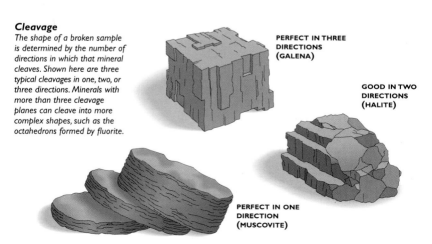

**PERFECT IN THREE
DIRECTIONS
(GALENA)**

**GOOD IN TWO
DIRECTIONS
(HALITE)**

**PERFECT IN ONE
DIRECTION
(MUSCOVITE)**

8 3

hackly (with little spikes or barbs), conchoidal (leaving a smooth shell-like surface), or splintery.

Fractured surfaces are generally easy to see, but cleavage planes are more difficult to identify. Sometimes a sample is obviously broken, with a cleavage plane cutting through the crystal; however, cleavage planes can be easily confused with the crystal faces themselves. In general, cleavage planes are not as perfectly smooth as crystal faces and they reflect light with a slightly different luster. In some instances, they are visible as cracks—referred to as "incipient" cleavage planes—within the sample.

### *Specific Gravity Test*
*To perform this test, you can use a hanging scale and a hook obtained from your local hardware store, or order a specially tooled balance available by catalog from geological supply stores.*

The upper left portion of a willemite sample fluoresces green under ultraviolet light. The red is calcite, which is white to the naked eye.

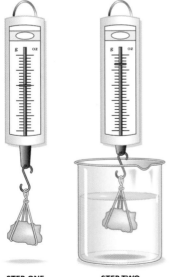

**STEP ONE**
Weigh the sample in air.

**STEP TWO**
Weigh the sample in water.

## SPECIFIC GRAVITY

Minerals have different densities. A piece of galena, which contains lead, weighs a great deal more than a piece of gypsum of the same size. Mineral density can be represented by a number referred to as specific gravity. It is based on a comparison of the mineral's weight to the weight of the same volume of water. Galena has a specific gravity of about 7.5—it weighs 7.5 times more than the same volume of water. Gypsum has a specific gravity of 2.32. Since each species has its own specific gravity, which never changes, it is a useful identification tool.

Specific gravity can be determined by weighing the sample in air, then in water. The difference is the weight of the displaced water, which is then divided by the weight of the sample. Experienced collectors can sometimes estimate a sample's density by holding it in their hand in a test known as hefting. Others need to hold a known mineral in one hand (often a metal) when they heft the unknown mineral.

## OTHER PROPERTIES

Many minerals react to certain acids. Apply a drop of hydrochloric acid to a sample of calcite, for example, and the surface will fizz or effervesce. (When testing with acid, be sure to wear goggles and gloves.)

Minerals that display colors when illuminated with ultraviolet (UV) light are called fluorescent, a phenomenon named for fluorite, which shows this property strongly. A mineral that continues to glow after the light source is removed is termed phosphorescent, a property named for phosphorus. (Phosphorus doesn't actually phosphoresce, but produces light that has been likened to phosphorescence when it spontaneously combusts.) Some minerals fluoresce or phosphoresce under long-wave UV light, others under short wave; special lamps are available for both types. Not all samples of a fluorescent or phosphorescent mineral will fluoresce or phosphoresce, but if a sample does exhibit one of the properties, you can eliminate the many minerals that never do.

A mineral such as magnetite acts as a magnet—detected by moving a sample alongside a compass to see if the needle deflects. A mineral containing iron will be attracted by a magnet. A few minerals, such as uranium, show radioactivity, detectable by a Geiger counter.

Feel and smell also help in identification. Sulphur has a distinctive smell, talc a soapy feel. Venturesome collectors can experiment with more complicated tests, such as the borax bead test shown at right.

### Borax Bead Test

*The color of beads produced in this test can help identify certain minerals. Chromium produces a green bead; iron produces a paler bottle-green bead; copper produces a red-brown bead; nickel produces a gray bead; and manganese produces a colorless bead. Platinum wire is available at hardware stores and borax at most supermarkets.*

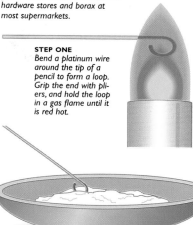

**STEP ONE**
Bend a platinum wire around the tip of a pencil to form a loop. Grip the end with pliers, and hold the loop in a gas flame until it is red hot.

**STEP TWO**
Dip the hot wire in some powdered borax.

**STEP THREE**
Heat the borax in the flame until it forms a colorless glassy bead.

**STEP FOUR**
Touch the borax bead to some powder of the mineral to be tested and heat the sample in the flame until it forms a bead. Let the bead cool and note its color.

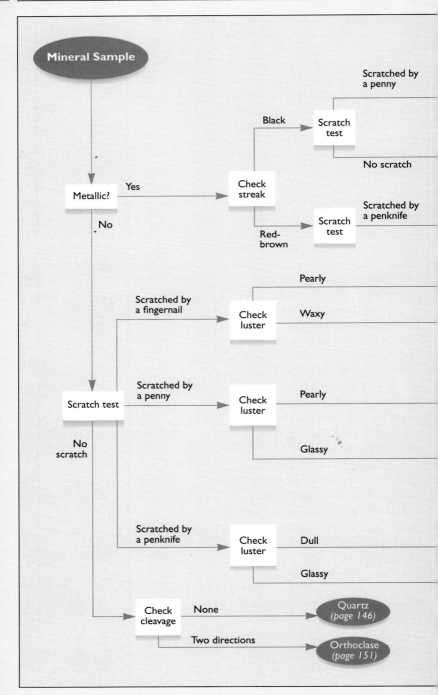

Mineral Sample

Metallic? — Yes → Check streak
- Black → Scratch test
  - Scratched by a penny
  - No scratch
- Red-brown → Scratch test
  - Scratched by a penknife

Metallic? — No → Scratch test
- Scratched by a fingernail → Check luster
  - Pearly
  - Waxy
- Scratched by a penny → Check luster
  - Pearly
  - Glassy
- Scratched by a penknife → Check luster
  - Dull
  - Glassy
- No scratch → Check cleavage
  - None → Quartz (page 146)
  - Two directions → Orthoclase (page 151)

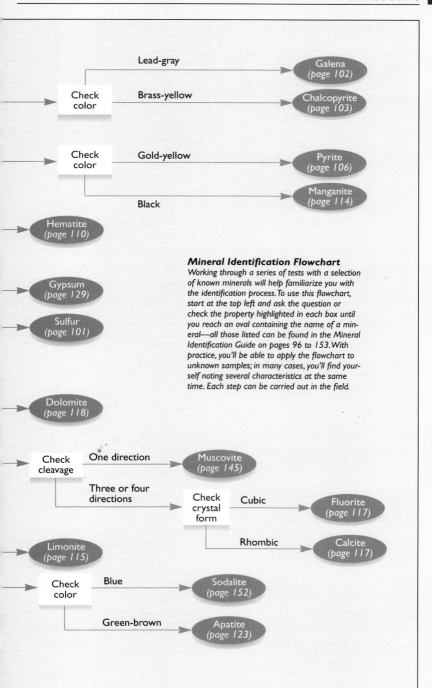

Lead-gray → Galena (page 102)

Check color

Brass-yellow → Chalcopyrite (page 103)

Check color

Gold-yellow → Pyrite (page 106)

→ Manganite (page 114)

Black

Hematite (page 110)

Gypsum (page 129)

Sulfur (page 101)

Dolomite (page 118)

### Mineral Identification Flowchart

Working through a series of tests with a selection of known minerals will help familiarize you with the identification process. To use this flowchart, start at the top left and ask the question or check the property highlighted in each box until you reach an oval containing the name of a mineral—all those listed can be found in the Mineral Identification Guide on pages 96 to 153. With practice, you'll be able to apply the flowchart to unknown samples; in many cases, you'll find yourself noting several characteristics at the same time. Each step can be carried out in the field.

Check cleavage — One direction → Muscovite (page 145)

Three or four directions →

Check crystal form — Cubic → Fluorite (page 117)

Rhombic → Calcite (page 117)

Limonite (page 115)

Check color — Blue → Sodalite (page 152)

Green-brown → Apatite (page 123)

# Identifying Rocks

Figuring out the identity of a rock sample is not a straightforward process. Even professional petrologists can't always make an identification until they examine thin slices of rock under a microscope to see the mineral composition and fine grain patterns. Review the checklist items below and apply your knowledge to some known rocks using the rock identification flowchart on pages 92 to 93. With practice, you'll learn to recognize most of the common rocks included in the guide *(pages 154-173)*.

The Valley of Fire in Nevada's Lake Meade National Recreation Area is the site of numerous weathered sandstone formations.

### GRAINS

Experienced rock hounds usually start identifying a rock by the size of its grains. The grains are the speckles and patches of contrasting colors and shininess that can be seen very clearly on some rocks. If the grains are readily visible, the rock is referred to as coarse-grained. When grains appear to be cemented tightly together, possibilities include a gneiss or a granite. When grains appear weakly cemented together, the rock could be a conglomerate or a breccia.

If you need a magnifying glass to see grains clearly, then the rock is classified as medium-grained. The possible choices include the various schists and a sandstone. If you notice that the grains—whether coarse or medium—are very tightly interlocked, the rock may be gabbro, gneiss, or marble.

If you cannot see the grains—even with a magnifying glass—then the rock is classified as fine-grained. Basalt and slate are examples of commonly found fine-grained rocks.

## Road Cuts for Rock Hounds

In constructing canals, railroads, and highways, engineers have cut into the Earth, exposing magnificent sedimentary sequences such as this one along I-40 at Kingman, Arizona. Rock hunters know that even the most prosaic road cut can hold an epic poem of fossils and minerals. The Interstate system offers unmatched pickings in the mountains and plateaus of the west. Few of these cuts are more than thirty years old, so they are virtually unweathered and unoxidized. From granite to quartz, rocks and minerals found in road cuts are easy to spot and excavate. Just make sure you stay well off the road.

### FOLIATION

Some metamorphic rocks, such as gneiss and schist, have visible foliation—wavy striations that ripple across their surface.

### MINERALS

Sometimes the minerals that make up a rock are visible. When looking at a piece of granite, for example, you can usually see glassy bits of quartz, creamy or pink bits of feldspar, and black flecks of mica biotite.

### TEXTURE

Overall appearance is a useful clue in some cases. The frothiness of pumice and the glassiness of obsidian are easy to spot, for instance.

### COLOR

Rocks come in a variety of colors— usually whites, grays, browns, or blacks. When iron is present—as in the case of ironstone and red

*A river in Yosemite, California, is strewn with a variety of rocks, including granite, basalt, chunks of volcanic ash, and sedimentary sandstones and shales.*

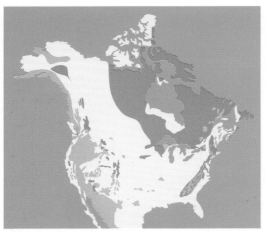

**Where the Rocks Are**
This map shows the major rock formations in North America.

SEDIMENTARY ROCK
IGNEOUS ROCK
METAMORPHIC ROCK

geological hammer; quartzite won't. It is much harder. Other unique features that distinguish certain rocks include the pinging sound slate makes when it is struck; the way shale separates into layers; the smooth shell-like fractures made by flint; and the crumbly chunks formed by mudstone when it breaks.

marl—the rock may take on a reddish hue. Some rocks appear in different shades, depending on the sample. Other rocks occur in one distinctive color that can help identify them—or at least narrow down the choices. For example, andesite can often be identified by its brownish-green color and diorite by its salt-and-pepper tones.

### FOSSILS

The presence of fossils signals that the rock is sedimentary—possibly shale, sandstone, or limestone.

### OTHER TELLTALE FEATURES

Sometimes the clue to a rock's identity lies in one particular feature. Quartz sandstone and quartzite, for example, are both yellowish, medium-grained rocks and can be confused. Quartz sandstone will crumble under a blow from a

### READING LANDSCAPE

Even with this checklist, amateur rock hounds will sometimes find it hard to distinguish one rock from another. When individual rock characteristics are insufficient to identify a particular rock, study the surrounding landscape. If you understand its geology, you are more likely to be able to identify the rock as sedimentary, igneous, or metamorphic.

Layers of rock exposed on a cliff face or a riverbank tell you you're probably looking at sedimentary rock. Tower shapes, such as the buttes of Monument Valley, on the border between Utah and Arizona, indicate the presence of sandstone. Rolling landscapes, peppered with caverns and water-filled sinkholes, point to the presence of limestone. In southeastern France, the Vercors region with its limestone cavern, Gouffre Berger, is one such example.

On volcanic islands, such as Hawaii or the Greek island of

*The Canadian Rockies are primarily made of limestones and shales. Hikers may find rocks here that contain marine fossils, evidence that the region where the rocks formed was once submerged in an ancient shallow sea.*

Santorini in the eastern Mediterranean, you'll see mostly volcanic igneous rock. Keep an eye out for mounds of tuff created by light, frothy-looking pumice and volcanic ash. Volcanic rock can also be found on the west coast of North America—on the slopes of Mount St. Helens, for instance. Farther south, the Sierra Nevada form one huge batholith, an igneous intrusion. To the east, the Rocky Mountains are a mix of rock types: primarily sedimentary in the north, but igneous and metamorphic as well in the south and west. Farther east, igneous rock is buried beneath sediments, except in a few spots in the central states—the Black Hills and the Ozarks, for instance—where the rock has been exposed by uplift and erosion. North and east, the

Canadian Shield is dominated by metamorphic rock, broken by remnants of plutonic intrusions.

Southward the landscape features distinctive ridges, called dikes and sills, of basalt. A dike forms when magma solidifies in a sheet that cuts across layers of rock. A sill is created when magma solidifies between two layers of rock. One widely recognized sill hems the Hudson River— a 550-foot (168-m) rampart known as the Palisades.

Not far away lie the Appalachian Mountains, once a towering backbone of sedimentary rock, but long since pressured into metamorphic rock—the sedimentary rock was squeezed so hard, in fact, that some of the material actually melted into magma and then recrystallized eons later as igneous rock.

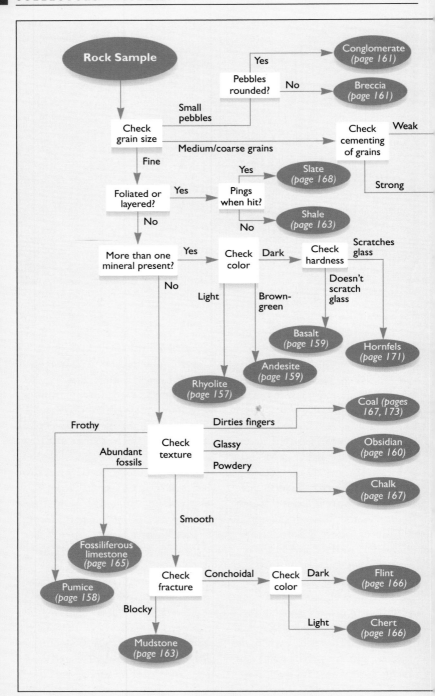

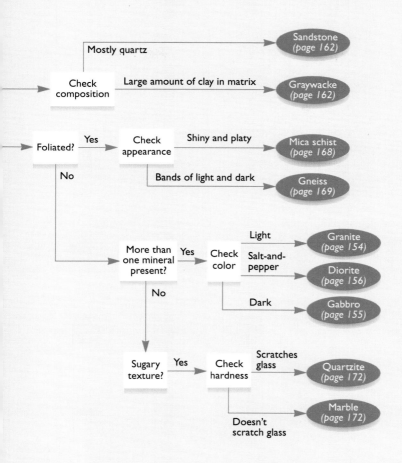

Mostly quartz → Sandstone (page 162)

Check composition

Large amount of clay in matrix → Graywacke (page 162)

Foliated? — Yes → Check appearance

Shiny and platy → Mica schist (page 168)

Bands of light and dark → Gneiss (page 169)

No

More than one mineral present? — Yes → Check color

Light → Granite (page 154)

Salt-and-pepper → Diorite (page 156)

Dark → Gabbro (page 155)

No

Sugary texture? — Yes → Check hardness

Scratches glass → Quartzite (page 172)

Doesn't scratch glass → Marble (page 172)

**Rock Identification Flowchart**
*Rock identification based on visual characteristics is quite tricky, but working through this flow-chart can help narrow down your choices. To work out whether your rock sample is one of the common rocks shown here, start at the top left of the chart. Check the various properties and answer the questions until you reach an oval with the name of a rock. Photographs of all the rocks mentioned here are contained in the Rock Identification Guide on pages 154 to 173.*

# IDENTIFICATION GUIDE

*Novice collectors will find it helpful to use this guide
in conjunction with the identification flowcharts for minerals
(page 86) and rocks (page 92)
and the mineral identification chart (page 178).*

For most rock and mineral collectors, the joy of collecting derives as much from learning about the pieces in the collection as it does from their actual acquisition. Being able to recognize a mineral by sight and understand how it was formed deepens the appreciation of natural beauty.

Of the thousands of minerals and rocks that make up this planet, more than 150 have been included in the following beginner's guide. Once you've become familiar with them, you may want to consult a

field guide designed for experienced collectors. Among the minerals and rocks profiled here, some were chosen because they're very common, such as sandstone and apatite. Others were selected because they play an important role in our society; examples include galena, a source of lead, and granite, the ubiquitous building material. Still other minerals and rocks have been included because of their special interest to collectors; the gemstones ruby and sapphire belong to this category. Finally there are those,

MINERAL NAME — CHEMICAL FORMULA OF MINERAL — MINERAL FAMILY

**SILVER** | Ag                                  *Native Element*

| | |
|---|---|
| **Crystal System:** Isometric | |
| **Color:** Silver-white; tarnishes to black | |
| **Transparency:** Opaque | |
| **Luster:** Metallic | |
| **Streak:** Silver-white | |
| **Hardness:** 2.5 to 3.0 | |
| **Habit:** Wiry, scaly, platy, or dendritic; twinning common | |
| **Cleavage:** N/A | |
| **Fracture:** Hackly | |
| **Specific Gravity:** 10.0 to 11.0 | |
| **Tests:** Soluble in nitric acid | |

BRIEF DESCRIPTION OF MINERAL, INCLUDING ITS USE, MINERAL ENVIRONMENT, AND OCCURRENCE.

KEY FACTS ABOUT MINERAL

A malleable and ductile mineral that rarely forms crystals, silver has the highest thermal and electrical conductivity of any known substance. Renowned twisted-wire silver specimens from Kongsberg, Norway, can measure as much as a foot long and as thick as a man's wrist. **USE:** Used to make coins, jewelry, tableware; in photography; in dentistry; in electroplating; and as a catalyst. **ENVIRONMENT:** In hydrothermal veins and in the oxidized zone of ore deposits; usually associated with other silver-bearing minerals. **OCCURRENCE:** Found worldwide, notably in western U.S.; Canada; Mexico; Chile; Australia.

such as the silicates olivine, quartz, and tourmaline, that fit two or more of the criteria.

Most of the terms used to describe the rocks and minerals have been explained in previous chapters. If in doubt about the meaning of term, check the glossary on pages 182 to 185. The Mineral Identification Guide *(pages 96-153)* has been organized according to a modified version of Dana's *A System of Mineralogy,* a classification system that was first devised in 1837 when its author, American geologist James Dwight Dana, was only twenty-four years old *(page 49).* One of several important classification systems, Dana's is widely used across North America. The rocks in the Rock Identification Guide *(pages 154-173)* have been grouped according to whether they are igneous, sedimentary, or metamorphic.

**ROCK NAME**

**ROCK TYPE**

**DIORITE**                              *Igneous*

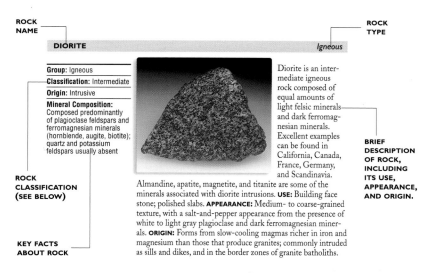

**Group:** Igneous

**Classification:** Intermediate

**Origin:** Intrusive

**Mineral Composition:** Composed predominantly of plagioclase feldspars and ferromagnesian minerals (hornblende, augite, biotite); quartz and potassium feldspars usually absent

**ROCK CLASSIFICATION (SEE BELOW)**

**KEY FACTS ABOUT ROCK**

Diorite is an intermediate igneous rock composed of equal amounts of light felsic minerals and dark ferromagnesian minerals. Excellent examples can be found in California, Canada, France, Germany, and Scandinavia.

**BRIEF DESCRIPTION OF ROCK, INCLUDING ITS USE, APPEARANCE, AND ORIGIN.**

Almandine, apatite, magnetite, and titanite are some of the minerals associated with diorite intrusions. **USE:** Building face stone; polished slabs. **APPEARANCE:** Medium- to coarse-grained texture, with a salt-and-pepper appearance from the presence of white to light gray plagioclase and dark ferromagnesian minerals. **ORIGIN:** Forms from slow-cooling magmas richer in iron and magnesium than those that produce granites; commonly intruded as sills and dikes, and in the border zones of granite batholiths.

| CLASSIFICATION | | |
|---|---|---|
| **ROCK** | **CRITERIA** | **CATEGORIES** |
| **IGNEOUS** | Amount of silica present: | • Acidic: More than 65 percent silica<br>• Intermediate: From 55 to 65 percent silica<br>• Basic: From 45 to 55 percent silica<br>• Ultrabasic: Less than 45 percent silica |
| **SEDIMENTARY** | Composition of rock-forming sediment: | • Detrital: Formed of fragments from pre-existing rocks<br>• Chemical: Formed by chemical processes<br>• Biochemical: Formed by biochemical processes<br>• Organic: Formed of grains from organic matter |
| **METAMORPHIC** | Type of metamorphism; may be low-, medium-, or high-grade depending on intensity of heat and/or pressure: | • Contact: Involves heat alone<br>• Regional: Involves heat and pressure |

# Mineral Identification Guide

Arranged according to the modified Dana system, the following mineral profiles contain the key facts you need to identify your mineral samples.

**GOLD** | *Au* *Native Element*

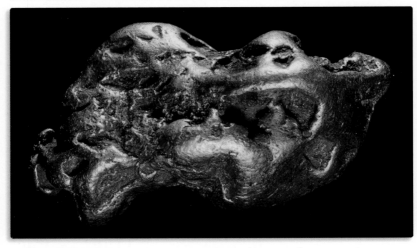

| | |
|---|---|
| **Crystal System:** Isometric | |
| **Color:** Gold-yellow (pure) | |
| **Transparency:** Opaque | |
| **Luster:** Metallic | |
| **Streak:** Gold-yellow | |
| **Hardness:** 2.2 to 3.0 | |
| **Habit:** Massive/granular, scaly, dendritic, or platy | |
| **Cleavage:** N/A | |
| **Fracture:** Hackly | |
| **Specific Gravity:** 19.3 (pure) | |
| **Tests:** Insoluble in acids other than aqua regia | |

Gold is present in the Earth's crust and in seawater in amounts of about six parts per hundred million. Nearly all gold is found in its native (pure) state. Sometimes gold is confused with pyrite, chalcopyrite, or biotite (especially if partially weathered and wet). But pyrite is harder, chalcopyrite is soft and brittle, and biotite is flaky. Gold is silvery white when alloyed with a high content of silver, orange-red when alloyed with copper. **USE:** Because of its malleability, gold has been used since ancient times to make jewelry and ornaments. It is also used in dentistry because of its inert nature—in most instances, it doesn't react with mouth fluids. Gold is the international standard for world finance. **ENVIRONMENT:** Usually found in hydrothermal veins, often in association with quartz; in placer or alluvial deposits; and in consolidated alluvial deposits. **OCCURRENCE:** Western U.S., notably Nevada, California, Alaska; Canada; Russia; Mexico; Chile; Witwatersrand district in Transvaal, Africa.

## SILVER | Ag — *Native Element*

**Crystal System:** Isometric

**Color:** Silver-white; tarnishes to black

**Transparency:** Opaque

**Luster:** Metallic

**Streak:** Silver-white

**Hardness:** 2.5 to 3.0

**Habit:** Wiry, scaly, platy, or dendritic; twinning common

**Cleavage:** N/A

**Fracture:** Hackly

**Specific Gravity:** 10.0 to 11.0

**Tests:** Soluble in nitric acid

A malleable and ductile mineral that rarely forms crystals, silver has the highest thermal and electrical conductivity of any known substance. Renowned twisted-wire silver specimens from Kongsberg, Norway, can measure as much as a foot long and as thick as a man's wrist. **USE:** Used to make coins, jewelry, tableware; in photography; in dentistry; in electroplating; and as a catalyst. **ENVIRONMENT:** In hydrothermal veins and in the oxidized zone of ore deposits; usually associated with other silver-bearing minerals. **OCCURRENCE:** Found worldwide, notably in western U.S.; Canada; Mexico; Chile; Australia.

## COPPER | Cu — *Native Element*

**Crystal System:** Isometric

**Color:** Copper-red; tarnishes to green, blue, and black

**Transparency:** Opaque

**Luster:** Metallic

**Streak:** Copper-red

**Hardness:** 2.5 to 3.0

**Habit:** Scaly, platy, or dendritic

**Cleavage:** N/A

**Fracture:** Hackly

**Specific gravity:** 8.9

**Tests:** Soluble in nitric acid

Copper is abundant enough to be mined in its native (pure) form only on the Keweenaw Peninsula in northern Michigan and in Coro-Coro, Bolivia. Usually it is mined from copper-rich ores such as chalcopyrite and bornite. It rarely forms crystals. **USE:** A good conductor, copper is widely used for electrical wiring. Ductile and malleable, it is rolled and shaped to make water pipes. It is also mixed with other metals—for example, with zinc to make brass; with tin to make bronze. **ENVIRONMENT:** Forms in cavities and fissures of basalt volcanic rocks. **OCCURRENCE:** Found in association with other elements, such as silver and iron. Beautiful specimens have been discovered in New Mexico, Michigan, Arizona; Canada; Chile; Peru; southwestern Australia; Zambia.

## PLATINUM | *Pt* — *Native Element*

**Crystal System:** Isometric

**Color:** Whitish steel-gray to dark gray

**Transparency:** Opaque

**Luster:** Metallic

**Streak:** Steel gray

**Hardness:** 4.0 to 4.5

**Habit:** Crystals rare; usually granular, scaly, or in nuggets, sometimes dendritic

**Cleavage:** N/A

**Fracture:** Hackly

**Specific Gravity:** 21.46 (pure); 14.0 to 19.0

Platinum has sometimes been called "white gold" because of its color; however, it is rarer than gold and worth much more. Platinum always contains iron—up to as much as 28 percent. One of the largest platinum nuggets ever found weighed twenty-six pounds (11.8 kg). **USE:** Largest single use is in making automobile catalytic converters; also used in the electrical industries and in the manufacture of laboratory crucibles. **ENVIRONMENT:** Normally in placer or in igneous rocks in association with chromite, olivine, and magnetite; sometimes in contact metamorphic deposits and quartz veins. **OCCURRENCE:** In the gold sands of Trinity County, California; Platinum, Alaska; Sudbury, Ontario; Ireland; Russia; Brazil; Australia; Bushveld igneous complex in Transvaal, Africa.

## NICKEL-IRON | *NiFe* — *Native Element*

**Crystal System:** Isometric

**Color:** Steel-gray to black

**Transparency:** Opaque

**Luster:** Metallic

**Streak:** Gray

**Hardness:** 4.5

**Habit:** Massive/granular

**Cleavage:** Poor

**Fracture:** Hackly

**Specific Gravity:** 7.3 to 7.9

**Tests:** Strongly magnetic

Iron was known to the ancient Greeks, who considered it precious and rare. Native (pure) iron is seldom found in terrestrial rocks; it occurs mostly where volcanic rocks cut through coal seams. Nickel-iron is the major native metallic mineral found in meteorites. **USE:** Nickel-iron alloys are used to make cores of transformers. **ENVIRONMENT:** Found in carbonaceous sedimentary deposits and (rarely) in basalts; in small amounts in some placer deposits. **OCCURRENCE:** New Jersey, Missouri; Ontario; Ireland; Scotland; France; in large masses at Disko Island, Greenland.

## MERCURY | *Hg*                                    *Native Element*

| | |
|---|---|
| **Crystal System:** Hexagonal | |
| **Color:** Tin-white | |
| **Transparency:** Opaque | |
| **Luster:** Brilliant metallic | |
| **Streak:** N/A | |
| **Hardness:** N/A | |
| **Habit:** Liquid; forms rhombohedral crystals at -38.2°F (-39.0°C) | |
| **Cleavage:** N/A | |
| **Fracture:** N/A | |
| **Specific Gravity:** 14.5 | |
| **Tests:** Soluble in nitric acid | |

Mercury is known as "quicksilver" for its color and because the metal can roll across any surface without wetting it. Mercury is the only metal that is liquid under normal conditions. **USE:** Mercury's low boiling point has made it a valuable ingredient in scientific instruments. **ENVIRONMENT:** As small globules in cinnabar near recent volcanic rocks or as deposits from certain hot springs. **OCCURRENCE:** Coast Range, California; Terlingua, Texas; Almaden, Spain; Mexico; China.

## ARSENIC | *As*                                    *Native Element*

| | |
|---|---|
| **Crystal Systems:** Trigonal | |
| **Color:** Light gray | |
| **Transparency:** Opaque | |
| **Luster:** Submetallic | |
| **Streak:** Light gray | |
| **Hardness:** 3.5 | |
| **Habit:** Massive/granular, globular, or stalactitic | |
| **Cleavage:** Perfect in one direction | |
| **Fracture:** Uneven | |
| **Specific Gravity:** 5.6 to 5.8 | |

Arsenic is derived from a Greek word that means masculine. It gives off a garlicky odor when heated. **USE:** To make gallium arsenides, used to manufacture computer chips in many ways superior to silicon chips. **ENVIRONMENT:** In hydrothermal veins, usually in igneous or metamorphic rocks; often in association with silver, cobalt, or nickel ores. **OCCURRENCE:** Inyo, Monterey, Nevada counties in California; Louisiana; Santa Cruz County, Arizona; Alder Island, British Columbia; Quebec; New Brunswick; Germany; Italy; Mexico; Copoapó, Chile; Peru; Australia; South Africa.

## BISMUTH | *Bi*         *Native Element*

**Crystal System:** Trigonal

**Color:** Silver-white with pinkish to reddish tint (darkens with exposure); tarnishes iridescent

**Transparency:** Opaque

**Luster:** Metallic

**Streak:** Silver-white; shiny

**Hardness:** 2 to 2.5

**Habit:** Crystals rare; massive/granular or arborescent; twinning common

**Cleavage:** Good in one direction across crystal length

**Fracture:** Conchoidal

**Specific Gravity:** 9.7 to 9.8

**Tests:** Globule formed when melted soluble in nitric acid

Bismuth has been found in Moon rocks. Sometimes as it forms, its edges and corners grow preferentially, resulting in hollowed-out crystals called hopper crystals. **USE:** Important ingredient of low-melting alloys used for fire-detection equipment; also used in pharmaceuticals. **ENVIRONMENT:** In hydrothermal veins, in association with ores of gold, silver, tin, nickel, cobalt, or lead; in pegmatites, quartz veins, and placer deposits. **OCCURRENCE:** San Diego County, California; Colorado; Chesterfield district, South Carolina; Cobalt district, Ontario; Great Bear Lake, Northwest Territories; England; Bolivia; South Africa; Australia.

## ANTIMONY | *Sb*         *Native Element*

**Crystal Systems:** Trigonal

**Color:** White to gray

**Transparency:** Opaque

**Luster:** Brilliant metallic

**Streak:** Gray

**Hardness:** 3.0 to 3.5

**Habit:** Crystals rare; massive/granular or globular; twinning common

**Cleavage:** Perfect in one direction

**Fracture:** Uneven

**Specific Gravity:** 6.6 to 6.7

Most antimony comes from stibnite and antimonial lead ores. Refined antimony is often called "star" antimony because of the fernlike surface markings developed during the process. **USE:** Fireworks (powdered antimony burns with a blue flame); safety-match heads and strikers; to harden lead. **ENVIRONMENT:** In hydrothermal veins, often in association with silver, silver ores, arsenic, sphalerite, pyrite, galena, or quartz. **OCCURRENCE:** Kern County in California; Quebec; New Brunswick; Mexico; Chile; South Africa.

## SULFUR | S
*Native Element*

**Crystal System:** Orthorhombic

**Color:** Bright yellow to yellowish brown; sometimes gray, reddish, or greenish

**Transparency:** Transparent to translucent

**Luster:** Resinous to greasy

**Streak:** White

**Hardness:** 1.5 to 2.5

**Habit:** Tabular, stalactitic masses, granular, fibrous, or earthy; twinning rare

**Cleavage:** Poor in two directions

**Fracture:** Conchoidal to uneven

**Specific Gravity:** 2.0 to 2.1

**Tests:** Insoluble in water, unaffected by most acids; soluble in carbon disulfide and some oils

Sulfur exists in several forms, including the ordinary, yellow, orthorhombic alpha form, which is stable below 204°F (95.6°C). **USE:** Sulfuric acid; gunpowder, fireworks; in bleaching; and in vulcanizing rubber. **ENVIRONMENT:** Sulfur-forming bacteria produce sulfur. Only a few salt domes hold commercial deposits of sulfur, but the ones that do contain millions of tons. Sulfur occurs as encrusting masses around volcanic vents or hot springs; in sedimentary rocks—principally limestones associated with gypsum; in cap rocks of salt domes with anhydrite, gypsum, and calcite; rarely as secondary mineral in ore deposits. **OCCURRENCE:** Salt domes of Louisiana, Texas; Hawaii; California; Chile; Argentina. Spectacular crystals have been found in Sicily and Mexico.

## DIAMOND | C
*Native Element*

**Crystal System:** Isometric

**Color:** Colorless; may be white to blue-white, yellow, brown, pink, red, or black

**Transparency:** Usually transparent, can be translucent, rarely opaque; sometimes strongly fluorescent

**Luster:** Adamantine; uncut crystals appear greasy

**Streak:** White

**Hardness:** 10.0

**Habit:** Mostly octahedral crystals, often flattened and etched; rarer as cubes with curved faces; sometimes twinned

**Cleavage:** Perfect in four directions

**Fracture:** Conchoidal

**Specific Gravity:** 3.5

Diamond is the hardest natural substance. The name comes from the Greek word *adamas*, meaning invincible. The color and transparency of diamonds vary and have a considerable impact on their value. Many so-called diamonds, such as the Arkansas, Herkimer, and Bristol, are in fact rock crystals—quartz. **USE:** Jewelry; surgery, especially on the eye; industrial diamonds, usually called bort, are used in drill bits, in fine-grinding and polishing, and in dies for drawing very fine wire. **ENVIRONMENT:** Found in kimberlite and in alluvial deposits; rarely in meteorites. **OCCURRENCE:** Murfreesboro in Pike County, Arkansas; Kelsey Lake Mine, Colorado; St. Helen's Island in Montreal, Quebec; Northwest Territories; Russia; Africa, especially Zaire, South Africa; Brazil; Venezuela; Australia.

## GRAPHITE | C *Native Element*

| | |
|---|---|
| **Crystal System:** Hexagonal | |
| **Color:** Black to steel-gray | |
| **Transparency:** Opaque | |
| **Luster:** Dull metallic | |
| **Streak:** Black | |
| **Hardness:** 1.0 to 2.0 | |
| **Habit:** Flat, tabular, hexagonal crystals, may show triangular striations; massive, foliated, or columnar | |
| **Cleavage:** Perfect in one direction | |
| **Fracture:** Conchoidal | |
| **Specific Gravity:** 2.1 to 2.3 | |
| **Tests:** Insoluble in acids | |

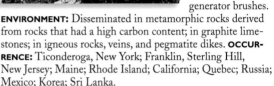

The name comes from the Greek word *graphein*, meaning to write. **USE:** Pencils; because of its high melting temperature—5,432°F (3,000°C)—in foundry facings, crucibles, electrodes, lubricants, paints, generator brushes. **ENVIRONMENT:** Disseminated in metamorphic rocks derived from rocks that had a high carbon content; in graphite limestones; in igneous rocks, veins, and pegmatite dikes. **OCCURRENCE:** Ticonderoga, New York; Franklin, Sterling Hill, New Jersey; Maine; Rhode Island; California; Quebec; Russia; Mexico; Korea; Sri Lanka.

## GALENA | PbS *Sulfide*

| | |
|---|---|
| **Crystal System:** Isometric | |
| **Color:** Lead-gray | |
| **Transparency:** Opaque | |
| **Luster:** Metallic | |
| **Streak:** Lead-gray | |
| **Hardness:** 2.5 | |
| **Habit:** Massive, splintery; sometimes twinned | |
| **Cleavage:** Perfect in three directions at ninety degrees | |
| **Fracture:** Even (rarely seen) | |
| **Specific Gravity:** 7.4 to 7.6 | |
| **Tests:** Reacts with hydrochloric acid to produce odor of rotten eggs | |

The name galena comes from the Latin word *galena*, for lead ore. It sometimes oxidizes to anglesite, cerussite, pyromorphite, or mimetite. **USE:** Galena is the most important lead ore and a good source of silver. **ENVIRONMENT:** Widely distributed in sedimentary rock; in hydrothermal veins in association with a variety of minerals, including sphalerite, pyrite, chalcopyrite, quartz, dolomite, fluorite; less frequently in pegmatites. **OCCURRENCE:** Joplin, Missouri; Colorado; Utah; Tennessee; California; Cornwall, Cumberland, England; Scotland; Broken Hill, Australia.

## SPHALERITE | $(Zn, Fe)S$                            *Sulfide*

**Crystal System:** Isometric

**Color:** Yellow, brown, red, green, or black

**Transparency:** Transparent to translucent; can appear opaque

**Luster:** Resinous; opaque specimens metallic

**Streak:** Reddish brown (dark varieties) to light yellow or white

**Hardness:** 3.5 to 4.0

**Habit:** Usually massive, coarse to fine granular; twinning common

**Cleavage:** Perfect in six directions

**Fracture:** Conchoidal

**Specific Gravity:** 3.9 to 4.1

**Tests:** Dissolves in warm hydrochloric acid

Sphalerite is known by a variety of names, such as zinc blende or black jack (referring to its black variety). As its iron content increases, it grows darker in color. Its name comes from the Greek word *sphaleros*, meaning treacherous, because of its variable color. Under certain conditions, sphalerite alters to limonite, hemimorphite, and smithsonite. **USE:** The most common zinc ore; an important source of the rare elements cadmium, indium, gallium, and germanium. **ENVIRONMENT:** Hydrothermal veins associated with galena; limestone associated with pyrite, pyrrhotite, and magnetite. **OCCURRENCE:** Large deposits in Joplin, Missouri; Franklin, New Jersey. Beautiful crystals have been discovered in Binnenthal, Switzerland; Picos de Europa, Spain. Also found in Canada; Mexico; China.

## CHALCOPYRITE | $CuFeS_2$                         *Sulfide*

**Crystal System:** Tetragonal

**Color:** Brass-yellow, often with iridescent tarnish

**Transparency:** Opaque

**Luster:** Metallic

**Streak:** Greenish black

**Hardness:** 3.5 to 4.0

**Habit:** Massive or compact; sometimes twinned

**Cleavage:** Very poor

**Fracture:** Conchoidal to uneven

**Specific Gravity:** 4.1 to 4.3

**Tests:** Soluble in nitric acid

Chalcopyrite is also known as copper pyrite, its chemical formula being that of pyrite with copper added. The name chalcopyrite comes from the Greek words *chalkos*, for brass, and *pyrites*, for fiery. Under certain conditions, it alters to chalcocite, covellite, chryscolla, and malachite. **USE:** It is the most common and most important copper ore. **ENVIRONMENT:** In hydrothermal veins associated with pyrite, pyrrhotite, cassiterite, sphalerite, galena, quartz, calcite, and dolomite. Porphyry copper deposits contain chalcopyrite, pyrite, and bornite in small veins in igneous intrusions of quartz diorite or diorite porphyry. **OCCURRENCE:** Bingham, Utah; Butte, Montana; Chester County, Pennsylvania; Arizona; New Mexico; Sudbury, Ontario; Rouyn district, Quebec; Cornwall, England; Falhun, Sweden; Rio Tinto, Spain; Mexico.

## PYRRHOTITE | $Fe_{1-x}S$       *Sulfide*

| | |
|---|---|
| **Crystal System:** Monoclinic or hexagonal | |
| **Color:** Bronze-yellow; tarnishes to reddish brown | |
| **Transparency:** Opaque | |
| **Luster:** Metallic | |
| **Streak:** Grayish black | |
| **Hardness:** 3.5 to 4.5 | |
| **Habit:** Platy or tabular crystals (rare), striated faces; usually massive/granular or compact | |
| **Cleavage:** N/A | |
| **Fracture:** Uneven | |
| **Specific Gravity:** 4.6 to 4.7 | |

Pyrrhotite comes from the Greek word *pyrrhotes*, meaning reddish, referring to its oxidized color. It is noticeably magnetic, although less so than magnetite, the other common magnetic mineral. Pyrrhotite rarely forms crystals. **USE:** Important for its association with nickel (especially in Sudbury, Ontario). **ENVIRONMENT:** As disseminated grains in igneous rocks such as gabbro, associated with chalcopyrite, pentlandite, and pyrite; also in contact metamorphic deposits and in veins. **OCCURRENCE:** Lancaster County, Pennsylvania; Homestake Mine, Lead, South Dakota; Sudbury, Ontario; Chihuahua, Mexico; Minas Gerais, Brazil.

## CINNABAR | $HgS$       *Sulfide*

| | |
|---|---|
| **Crystal System:** Hexagonal | |
| **Color:** Vermilion to brownish red | |
| **Transparency:** Transparent to opaque | |
| **Luster:** Adamantine | |
| **Streak:** Vermilion to brownish red | |
| **Hardness:** 2.0 to 2.5 | |
| **Habit:** Massive/granular | |
| **Cleavage:** Perfect in three directions | |
| **Fracture:** Uneven | |
| **Specific Gravity:** 8.0 to 8.2 | |

Cinnabar is the only known ore of mercury. Its name comes from the Greek *kinnabaris*, which may derive from the Arabic *zinjafr* or the Persian *zinjifrah*, meaning dragon's blood. It is poisonous due to its mercury content and should be handled with care. **USE:** Mercury's low boiling point has made cinnabar a valuable ingredient in scientific instruments. It is also used to manufacture drugs, insecticides, and detonators for explosives. **ENVIRONMENT:** Found in association with native mercury, stibnite, realgar, arsenic, and antimony. Usually deposited near hot springs or sites of volcanic activity; also found in shallow mineral veins in association with calcite, chalcedony, opal, and quartz. **OCCURRENCE:** Western U.S., Almaden, Spain; Mexico; China.

## REALGAR | AsS
*Sulfide*

| | |
|---|---|
| **Crystal System:** Monoclinic | |
| **Color:** Red to orange-yellow | |
| **Transparency:** Transparent to translucent | |
| **Luster:** Resinous | |
| **Streak:** Orange-red | |
| **Hardness:** 1.0 to 1.5 | |
| **Habit:** Prismatic, striated; massive/granular, earthy | |
| **Cleavage:** Good in one direction | |
| **Fracture:** Conchoidal | |
| **Specific Gravity:** 3.5 | |

The name comes from the Arabic word *rahj al-gar*, which means powder of the mine, because realgar was originally found in a silver mine. With long exposure, realgar breaks down into a yellow powder, the mineral orpiment. **USE:** When mixed with saltpeter, it produces a brilliant white light in fireworks; no longer used as a pigment because of its poisonous nature. **ENVIRONMENT:** Found in small amounts in hydrothermal veins containing orpiment and other arsenic minerals; less frequently around hot springs, in limestones, and in dolomites. **OCCURRENCE:** Humbolt County, Nevada; Toole County, Utah; Kern County, California; Washington; Binnenthal, Switzerland; Felysobanya, Nagyag, Romania; Hunan, China.

## ORPIMENT | Ag₂S₃
*Sulfide*

| | |
|---|---|
| **Crystal System:** Monoclinic | |
| **Color:** Lemon-yellow to brownish or reddish yellow | |
| **Transparency:** Transparent to translucent | |
| **Luster:** Resinous; pearly on cleavage surfaces | |
| **Streak:** Pale yellow | |
| **Hardness:** 1.0 to 1.5 | |
| **Habit:** Usually massive/granular, foliated | |
| **Cleavage:** Good in one direction | |
| **Fracture:** N/A | |
| **Specific Gravity:** 3.4 to 3.5 | |

The name is derived from the Latin *auripigmentum*, or golden paint, because orpiment was believed to contain gold. **USE:** Once used as a pigment, but no longer because it is poisonous. **ENVIRONMENT:** Found with realgar in hydrothermal veins; also in hot spring deposits, usually with realgar and stibnite. **OCCURRENCE:** As nice crystals in Humbolt County, Nevada; as large crystals with calcite at Mercur, Toole County, Utah; Kern County, California; Yellowstone Park, Wyoming; Italy; Greece; Germany. Some of best crystals from Lukhumis, Georgia; China.

## STIBNITE | $Sb_2S_3$ — *Sulfide*

**Crystal System:** Orthorhombic

**Color:** Lead-gray; tarnishes iridescent

**Transparency:** Opaque

**Luster:** Metallic

**Streak:** Lead-gray to black

**Hardness:** 2.0

**Habit:** Striated, often bent, twisted, bladed, or radiating; needlelike

**Cleavage:** Perfect in one direction lengthwise

**Fracture:** Uneven

**Specific Gravity:** 4.5 to 4.6

**Tests:** Melts in match flame; ignites struck safety match

Stibnite is also known as "antimony glance." The name comes from the Greek word *stibi* or *stimmi*, for antimony. **USE:** The most common antimony ore. **ENVIRONMENT:** In hydrothermal veins, usually associated with quartz; as replacement ore bodies in limestone; in hot spring deposits. Often associated with realgar, orpiment, galena, pyrity, and cinnabar. **OCCURRENCE:** Coeur d'Alene district, Idaho; California; Oregon; Nevada; Cornwall, England; Felysobanya, Romania; Mexico; China. Some of the best crystals and crystal groups come from Ichinokawa, Japan.

## PYRITE | $FeS_2$ — *Sulfide*

**Crystal System:** Isometric

**Color:** Pale brass-yellow

**Transparency:** Opaque

**Luster:** Metallic

**Streak:** Greenish to brownish black

**Hardness:** 6.0 to 6.5

**Habit:** Cubic crystals common; striated, sometimes massive/granular or radiating; sometimes twinned

**Cleavage:** N/A

**Fracture:** Conchoidal to uneven

**Specific Gravity:** 4.9 to 5.2

**Tests:** May produce sparks when struck sharply with steel

The name comes from the Greek *pyr*, meaning fire; also known as fool's gold because it can be mistaken for gold. Pyrite can oxidize to limonite. **USE:** An important mineral because it is often found in association with gold and copper; also a good conductor of electricity. **ENVIRONMENT:** Found in different environments, including as an accessory mineral in igneous rocks; in black shales; as nodules; often as cubic crystals in metamorphic slates; in hydrothermal sulfide veins; and in contact metamorphic zones. **OCCURRENCE:** Chester, Vermont; Colorado; pyritized fossils in Lyme Regis, Dorset, England. Beautiful crystals in the Freiberg area, Germany; St. Gotthard, Switzerland. Exceptional crystals with hematite on Elba Island, Italy.

## ARSENOPYRITE | FeAsS

Sulfide

**Crystal System:** Monoclinic

**Color:** Silver gray-white; tarnishes brown

**Transparency:** Opaque

**Luster:** Metallic

**Streak:** Dark grayish black

**Hardness:** 5.5 to 6.0

**Habit:** Prismatic, often with striated faces; columnar, with rhombic cross-section; usually massive/granular, columnar, or compact; twinning common

**Cleavage:** Distinct in one direction

**Fracture:** Uneven

**Specific Gravity:** 5.9 to 6.2

Arsenopyrite comes from a contraction of its earlier name, arsenical pyrites, referring to its chemical similarity to pyrite, with the addition of arsenic. **USE:** The most common ore of arsenic. **ENVIRONMENT:** Found in hydrothermal veins; often associated with gold, tin ores, and silver as well as sphalerite, pyrite, chalcopyrite, galena, and quartz; also disseminated in sedimentary rocks, in gneiss, and in pegmatites. **OCCURRENCE:** Franconia, New Hampshire; Roxbury, Connecticut; Franklin, New Jersey; Deloro, Ontario; England; Norway; Portugal; France; Mexico; Japan.

## MOLYBDENITE | MoS₂

Sulfide

**Crystal System:** Hexagonal

**Color:** Pale bluish lead-gray

**Transparency:** Opaque

**Luster:** Metallic

**Streak:** Greenish gray; bluish gray on paper

**Hardness:** 1.0 to 1.5

**Habit:** Hexagonal tabular crystals; scaly, massive/granular, foliated

**Cleavage:** Perfect in one direction

**Fracture:** N/A

**Specific Gravity:** 4.6 to 4.8

Molybdenite comes from the Greek word *molybdos*, meaning lead. It has a greasy feel to the fingers and is sometimes confused with graphite. **USE:** An important ore for molybdenum. **ENVIRONMENT:** In small quantities in granites, pegmatites, and quartz veins; in contact metamorphic deposits associated with garnet, pyroxene, scheelite, pyrite, and tourmaline. **OCCURRENCE:** Climax Mine, Lake County, Colorado; Canada; Knaben Mine, Norway; Peru; Japan; Australia.

## SYLVANITE | $(Au,Ag)_2Te_4$ | Sulfide

| | |
|---|---|
| **Crystal System:** | Monoclinic |
| **Color:** | Steel-gray |
| **Transparency:** | Opaque |
| **Luster:** | Brilliant metallic |
| **Streak:** | Gray |
| **Hardness:** | 1.5 to 2.0 |
| **Habit:** | Prismatic, dendritic, bladed, columnar, or granular; sometimes twinned |
| **Cleavage:** | Perfect in one direction |
| **Fracture:** | Uneven |
| **Specific Gravity:** | 8.0 to 8.2 |

First discovered in Transylvania, its name derives from *sylvanium*, first proposed for the mineral tellurium, one of its elements. **USE:** Principal ore of gold and silver. **ENVIRONMENT:** A rare mineral found in hydrothermal veins in association with gold, pyrite, calavrite, quartz, and fluorite. **OCCURRENCE:** Cripple Creek district, Teller County, Colorado; Trinity County, California; Ontario; Romania; Guyana; Kalgoorlie, Mulgabbie, Australia.

## SKUTTERUDITE | $CoAs_{2-3}$ | Sulfide

| | |
|---|---|
| **Crystal System:** | Isometric |
| **Color:** | Tin-white to steel-gray; may show iridescent or grayish tarnish |
| **Transparency:** | Opaque |
| **Luster:** | Metallic |
| **Streak:** | Grayish black |
| **Hardness:** | 5.5 to 6.0 |
| **Habit:** | Crystals rare; massive/granular |
| **Cleavage:** | Indistinct in two directions |
| **Fracture:** | Uneven |
| **Specific Gravity:** | 5.7 to 6.9 |

Skutterudite is named for Skutterud, Norway, where it was discovered. It forms a series with nickel-skutterudite ($NiAs_{2-3}$) where nickel substitutes in the chemical structure for cobalt. **USE:** An ore of cobalt and nickel; cobalt oxide is used as a blue pigment in pottery and glassware. **ENVIRONMENT:** In association with cobaltite and nickeline veins. **OCCURRENCE:** Cobalt district, Ontario; Skutterud, Norway. Beautiful crystals from Irhtem, Morocco.

## ENARGITE | $Cu_3AsS_4$

*Sulfosalt*

| | |
|---|---|
| **Crystal System:** Orthorhombic | |
| **Color:** Dark gray to black | |
| **Transparency:** Opaque | |
| **Luster:** Metallic | |
| **Streak:** Black | |
| **Hardness:** 3.0 | |
| **Habit:** Massive/granular, bladed, or columnar; sometimes twinned | |
| **Cleavage:** Perfect in one direction; distinct in two other directions | |
| **Fracture:** Uneven | |
| **Specific Gravity:** 4.4 | |

The name enargite comes from *enargos*, a Greek word alluding to its excellent cleavage. **USE:** An ore of copper. **ENVIRONMENT:** Not common; found in near-surface deposits in association with chalcocite, bornite, covellite, pyrite, sphalerite, tetrahedrite, barite, and quartz. **OCCURRENCE:** Butte, Silver Bow County, Montana; Bingham County, Utah; Colorado; Nevada; California; Cerro de Pasco, Peru; Bolivia; Argentina; Philippine Islands; Tsumeb, Namibia.

## CUPRITE | $Cu_2^{+1}O$

*Oxide*

| | |
|---|---|
| **Crystal System:** Isometric | |
| **Color:** Red to dark red appearing almost black | |
| **Transparency:** Translucent to transparent (very thin pieces) | |
| **Luster:** Adamantine; sub-metallic to earthy | |
| **Streak:** Brownish red; shiny | |
| **Hardness:** 3.5 to 4.0 | |
| **Habit:** Cubic or octahedral crystals; massive/granular, earthy | |
| **Cleavage:** N/A | |
| **Fracture:** Uneven | |
| **Specific Gravity:** 5.8 to 6.1 | |
| **Tests:** Soluble in concentrated hydrochloric acid | |

Cuprite is named for *cuprum*, the Greek word for copper. Cuprite often alters to malachite. The variety chalcotrichite (also known as copper hair) is a needle-like form of cuprite. **USE:** An important ore of copper. **ENVIRONMENT:** Found in the oxidized zone of copper deposits in association with copper, malachite, azurite, and chalcocite. May be found coating copper. **OCCURRENCE:** Southwest U.S., especially Bisbee, Arizona; New Mexico. Notable malachite pseudomorphs in Chessy, France. Also in Chuquicamata, Chile; Mount Isa, Australia; Katanga, Congo; Namibia.

## CORUNDUM | $Al_2O_3$    *Oxide*

| | |
|---|---|
| **Crystal System:** Trigonal | |
| **Color:** White, gray, yellow, green, brown, purple to violet, blue (sapphire), or red (ruby) | |
| **Transparency:** Transparent to translucent | |
| **Luster:** Adamantine to glassy | |
| **Streak:** White | |
| **Hardness:** 9.0 | |
| **Habit:** Prismatic or tabular, often striated; twinning common | |
| **Cleavage:** N/A | |
| **Fracture:** Uneven to conchoidal | |
| **Specific Gravity:** 3.9 to 4.1 | |

*Ruby*

*Sapphire*

The name corundum derives from several words meaning ruby: *kuruntam* in Tamil, *kurivinda* in Sanskrit, and *karand* in Hindi. It is second only to diamond in hardness. Over the years, some of the varieties—for example, ruby, sapphire, and emery—have been given their own names; chemically they are the same. **USE:** As an ornamental stone; emery makes a good abrasive; non-gem-quality corundum has been used as bearings in watches. **ENVIRONMENT:** Found in nepheline syenite and nepheline syenite pegmatites; in marbles, gneiss, and schists; also in alluvial sands and gravels. **OCCURRENCE:** Finest gems from Burma; Sri Lanka. Emery found in Chester, Massachusetts; Naxos, Greece. Corundum also found in Montana; Colorado; Pennsylvania; North Carolina; Ontario; India; Afghanistan; Australia.

## HEMATITE | $Fe_2O_3$    *Oxide*

| | |
|---|---|
| **Crystal System:** Hexagonal | |
| **Color:** Red to reddish brown; steel-gray to black | |
| **Transparency:** Opaque | |
| **Luster:** Metallic to submetallic | |
| **Streak:** Brownish red | |
| **Hardness:** 5.0 to 6.0 | |
| **Habit:** Tabular crystals; compact, granular, radiating, globular, columnar, or platy | |
| **Cleavage:** N/A | |
| **Fracture:** Uneven to conchoidal | |
| **Specific Gravity:** 5.2 to 5.3 | |

The crushed powder of hematite creates a brownish-red pigment, once used to paint caves in the Pyrenees and to decorate the tombs of pharaohs. **USE:** Principal ore of iron; used to manufacture iron and steel; also finely ground to make jeweler's rouge. **ENVIRONMENT:** Found in large beds of sedimentary origin, in veins in igneous rocks, in metamorphic and contact-metamorphic rocks; associated with magnetite and as replacement deposits containing fluorite, barite, and calcite. **OCCURRENCE:** Deposits nearly one thousand feet (305 m) thick have been found in the Lake Superior regions of Minnesota, Michigan, Wisconsin. Also found in Canada; England; Norway; Switzerland. Spectacular six-inch (15-cm) crystals found in Brazil.

## ILMENITE | $Fe^{+2}TiO_3$

*Oxide*

**Crystal System:** Hexagonal

**Color:** Black

**Transparency:** Opaque

**Luster:** Submetallic to metallic

**Streak:** Black to brownish red

**Hardness:** 5.0 to 6.0

**Habit:** Tabular, granular, or compact; twinning common

**Cleavage:** N/A

**Fracture:** Conchoidal

**Specific Gravity:** 4.5 to 5.0

The name ilmenite comes from the Ilmen Mountains in Russia. The black beach sands in India and Florida are rich in ilmenite. It sometimes appears to be magnetic because it occurs intergrown with magnetite. **USE:** An important ore of titanium. **ENVIRONMENT:** As an accessory mineral in igneous rocks such as gabbro; sometimes in quartz veins with hematite and chalcopyrite; also in alluvial sands with magnetite, monazite, and rutile. **OCCURRENCE:** Adirondacks, New York; California; Arkansas; Massachusetts; Quebec; Krägerö, Norway; India; Australia.

## RUTILE | $TiO_2$

*Oxide*

**Crystal System:** Tetragonal

**Color:** Reddish brown; sometimes yellow, red, or black

**Transparency:** Transparent (thin pieces); dark varieties may be almost opaque

**Luster:** Adamantine; submetallic when dark colored

**Streak:** Pale brown

**Hardness:** 6.0 to 6.5

**Habit:** Striated, needlelike, massive; twinning common

**Cleavage:** Distinct, sometimes good, in two directions; poor in one direction

**Fracture:** Uneven

**Specific Gravity:** 4.2 to 4.4

Rutile comes from the Latin *rutilus*, which means red. Flèche d'amour is the name for rutilated quartz—quartz that contains needle-like crystals of rutile. **USE:** Important for its association with nickel (especially at Sudbury, Ontario); also used as a coating for welding rods. **ENVIRONMENT:** Found as an accessory mineral in a variety of igneous and metamorphic rocks, such as metamorphosed limestones and schists; as a secondary mineral arising from the breakdown of titanite; also found concentrated in alluvial deposits and beach sand. **OCCURRENCE:** California; South Dakota; Arkansas; Graves Mountain, Georgia; Sudbury, Ontario; Krägerö, Norway; Sweden; Germany; New South Wales, Queensland, Australia. Lovely samples of flèche d'amour found in Switzerland; Minas Gerais, Brazil.

## CASSITERITE | $SnO_2$ — *Oxide*

| | |
|---|---|
| **Crystal System:** | Tetragonal |
| **Color:** | Brown to black, red, or (rarely) yellow |
| **Transparency:** | Transparent to almost opaque |
| **Luster:** | Adamantine, sub-metallic, or glassy; greasy on fracture surface |
| **Streak:** | White to gray |
| **Hardness:** | 6.0 to 7.0 |
| **Habit:** | Pyramidal crystals; massive/granular or globular; twinning common |
| **Cleavage:** | Poor |
| **Fracture:** | Uneven |
| **Specific Gravity:** | 6.8 to 7.1 |

The name cassiterite comes from the Greek word *kassiteros*, meaning tin. Varieties include wood tin, which has a fibrous structure, and stream tin, which is often found in alluvial or placer deposits. Its specific gravity is unusually high for a mineral with a non-metallic luster. **USE:** Principal ore of tin. **ENVIRONMENT:** Usually found in hydrothermal veins, in pegmatites located near granite masses, and in alluvial deposits; often associated with wolframite, arsenopyrite, bismuthinite, topaz, quartz, and tourmaline. **OCCURRENCE:** Alaska; Washington; South Dakota; Cornwall, England; Germany; Namibia; Brazil; Bolivia; Indonesia; Malaysia; Australia; China.

## SPINEL | $MgAl_2O_4$ — *Oxide*

| | |
|---|---|
| **Crystal System:** | Isometric |
| **Color:** | Variable; usually red, but may be blue, green, brown, black, or colorless |
| **Transparency:** | Usually translucent, but ranges from transparent to nearly opaque |
| **Luster:** | Glassy to almost dull |
| **Streak:** | White; may be gray |
| **Hardness:** | 7.5 to 8.0 |
| **Habit:** | Octahedral crystals; massive, coarse granular, or compact; sometimes twinned |
| **Cleavage:** | N/A |
| **Fracture:** | Conchoidal |
| **Specific Gravity:** | 3.5 to 4.1 |

The name probably comes from the Latin word *spina*, meaning thorn, because of its sharp octahedral crystals. Pure spinel is colorless; the color variations are caused by minute amounts of trace elements. It forms a distinctive kind of twinning known as spinel twins. **USE:** As a less costly substitute for ruby. **ENVIRONMENT:** In gabbro as an accessory mineral; in association with phlogopite, graphite, and chondrodite in metamorphosed limestones; and, because of its hardness, as pebbles in river or beach sands. **OCCURRENCE:** New York; New Jersey; Canada; Finland; India; Burma; Sri Lanka.

## MAGNETITE | $Fe^{+2}Fe_2^{+3}O_4$ — *Oxide*

| | |
|---|---|
| **Crystal System:** Isometric | |
| **Color:** Iron to grayish black | |
| **Transparency:** Opaque | |
| **Luster:** Metallic to dull | |
| **Streak:** Black | |
| **Hardness:** 5.5 to 6.5 | |
| **Habit:** Octahedral crystals; massive/granular; twinning common | |
| **Cleavage:** None | |
| **Fracture:** Subconchoidal to uneven | |
| **Specific Gravity:** 5.2 | |

The name may come from Magnesia, Thessaly, a locality in Asia Minor, or from a fable about a shepherd, Magnes, who supposedly discovered the mineral on Mount Ida. Lodestone, or Hercules stone, is a variety that is magnetic; when suspended, it will act like a compass needle. **USE:** An important iron ore. **ENVIRONMENT:** As an accessory mineral in igneous and metamorphic rocks where, because of its relatively high specific gravity, it accumulates to form economically valuable deposits; in contact or regionally metamorphosed rocks; in hydrothermal veins; and, with corundum and spinel, in emery deposits. **OCCURRENCE:** Coast Range, California; Clark County, Paradise Range, Nevada; Magnet Cove, Arkansas; Canada; Mexico. Beautiful crystals found in Austria. Powerful natural magnets found in Germany; Siberia; the Bushfeld Complex, Transvaal.

## CHRYSOBERYL | $BeAl_2O_4$ — *Oxide*

| | |
|---|---|
| **Crystal System:** Orthorhombic | |
| **Color:** Shades of green and yellow | |
| **Transparency:** Translucent to transparent | |
| **Luster:** Glassy | |
| **Streak:** White | |
| **Hardness:** 8.5 | |
| **Habit:** Tabular, prismatic, or platy; twinning common | |
| **Cleavage:** Good in one direction; poor in two directions | |
| **Fracture:** Uneven to conchoidal | |
| **Specific Gravity:** 3.5 to 3.8 | |

The name comes from the Greek word *chrysos*, for golden yellow, referring to one of its colors. The variety alexandrite, named for Czar Alexander II of Russia, glows green in daylight and red in candlelight. It often contains small, needlelike, parallel inclusions. When cut as a cabochon (rounded top, flat bottom), this chrysoberyl reflects a moveable blue-white line of light, a phenomena called chatoyancy; the resulting gemstone is called a cat's-eye. **USE:** Popular as a gemstone. **ENVIRONMENT:** A rare mineral, chrysoberyl is almost always found as a crystal in granites, in pegmatites, in mica schists, and in alluvial sands and gravels. **OCCURRENCE:** Chester County, South Dakota; Golden, Colorado; Maine; New York. Gem crystals from Brazil; Burma. Some of the best Alexandrite from the Ural Mountains.

## MANGANITE | $Mn^{+3}O(OH)$ — Hydroxide

**Crystal System:** Monoclinic

**Color:** Dark steel-gray to black

**Transparency:** Opaque

**Luster:** Submetallic to dull

**Streak:** Reddish brown to black

**Hardness:** 4.0

**Habit:** Prismatic, often vertically striated with flat terminations; frequently grouped in bundles or as radiating aggregates; sometimes twinned

**Cleavage:** Perfect in one direction lengthwise

**Fracture:** Uneven

**Specific Gravity:** 4.2 to 4.4

**Tests:** Soluble in concentrated hydrochloric acid

The name refers to the mineral's manganese content. **USE:** An ore of manganese. **ENVIRONMENT:** In deposits precipitated from water and in hydrothermal veins, in association with pyrolusite, barite, and goethite. **OCCURRENCE:** Negaunee, Michigan; California; New Jersey; Georgia; Nova Scotia; Cornwall, England; Ilfeld, Harz Mountains, Ilmenau, Thuringia, Germany.

## DIASPORE | $AlO(OH)$ — Hydroxide

**Crystal System:** Orthorhombic

**Color:** Variable; colorless, white, gray, sometimes brown or pink

**Transparency:** Translucent

**Luster:** Glassy; pearly on cleavage surface

**Hardness:** 6.5 to 7.0

**Habit:** Platy, tabular, needlelike, massive, foliated, or scaly

**Cleavage:** Perfect in one direction

**Fracture:** Uneven

**Specific Gravity:** 3.2 to 3.5

The name comes from the Greek word *diaspheirein*, to scatter, referring to what happens to the mineral when it is heated. **USE:** As a refractory. **ENVIRONMENT:** Is usually found in metamorphosed limestones, with chlorite schists, and in large amounts in bauxite and aluminous clays; is associated with corundum, magnetite, and spinel in emery deposits. **OCCURRENCE:** Chester, Massachusetts; California; Arkansas; Missouri; Pennsylvania; Greenland; England; Norway; Turkey; Russia; Japan; China.

## GOETHITE | Fe<sup>+3</sup>O(OH)    *Hydroxide*

**Crystal System:**
Orthorhombic

**Color:** Reddish to dull yellow-brown (massive); brownish yellow (earthy)

**Transparency:** Opaque; sub-translucent in thin pieces

**Luster:** Adamantine (crystals); silky or dull (massive)

**Streak:** Brownish yellow

**Hardness:** 5.0 to 5.5

**Habit:** Crystals rare; needle-like, platy, compact, granular/massive, foliated, earthy

**Cleavage:** Perfect in one direction

**Fracture:** Uneven, splintery

**Specific Gravity:** 3.3 to 4.3

Goethite is named for Johann Wolfgang von Goethe, the eighteenth century German poet and mineral collector. It is produced by the weathering of iron-bearing minerals such as pyrite. Most of the material once labeled limonite is in fact goethite. **USE:** An important ore of iron, particularly in Europe. **ENVIRONMENT:** As a secondary mineral in the oxidized zones of hydrothermal veins containing iron-bearing minerals such as pyrite; also as a precipitate from water. The variety of goethite called bog iron ore precipitates from water in bogs or lagoons. **OCCURRENCE:** Nagaunee, Michigan; Appalachian Mountains; West Virginia; Tennessee; Alabama; Colorado; Cornwall, England; Cuba; Mexico; Brazil; Chile.

## LIMONITE    *Hydrous Iron Oxide*

**Crystal System:** N/A

**Color:** Dark to yellowish brown, red, yellow, or nearly black

**Transparency:** Opaque

**Luster:** Glassy to dull

**Streak:** Variable; brown to yellow

**Hardness:** Variable; up to 5.5

**Habit:** Massive; earthy

**Cleavage:** None

**Fracture:** Conchoidal to earthy

**Specific Gravity:** Variable; 2.7 to 4.3

The name limonite is a derivative of the Greek word *leimon*, meaning meadow; the mineral used to be called *wiesenerz*, for meadow ore or bog ore. Limonite is a general term for a group of brown, amorphous, naturally occurring hydrous iron oxides. Once thought to be a distinct mineral, limonite is a combination of minerals, mostly goethite. **USE:** A strong indicator of subsurface iron mineralization. **ENVIRONMENT:** A common secondary material formed by weathering of iron or iron-bearing minerals; may form as precipitate in bogs. **OCCURRENCE:** Connecticut; Massachusetts; New York; Germany; France; Ukraine; India; Cuba.

## BAUXITE

*Oxides & Hydroxides of Aluminum & Iron*

**Crystal System:** N/A

**Color:** Ocher-yellow, brown, red, or gray

**Transparency:** Opaque

**Luster:** Dull

**Streak:** White

**Hardness:** Variable; 1.0 to 3.0

**Habit:** Massive/granular, earthy, or pisolitic (pealike concretions)

**Cleavage:** N/A

**Fracture:** Earthy

**Specific Gravity:** 2.0 to 2.5

Like limonite, bauxite is widely used to describe a group of minerals. In this case, the mixture includes diaspore, gibbsite, boehmite, and other iron oxides. **USE:** An important ore of aluminum. **ENVIRONMENT:** Of secondary origin, bauxite minerals form under tropical conditions by long-term weathering of rocks containing aluminum silicates; the weathering and leaching removes the silica, leaving behind the much softer aluminum hydroxides. **OCCURRENCE:** Chester, Massachusetts (where diaspore within bauxite occurs as light purple crystals); Arkansas; Jamaica; Brazil; French Guiana.

## HALITE | *NaCl*

*Halide*

**Crystal System:** Isometric

**Color:** Colorless, white, reddish, yellow, or blue

**Transparency:** Transparent to translucent

**Luster:** Glassy

**Streak:** White

**Hardness:** 2.5

**Habit:** Cubic crystals, often with concave faces (hopper crystals); massive/granular or compact

**Cleavage:** Perfect in three directions at ninety degrees

**Fracture:** Conchoidal

**Specific Gravity:** 2.1 to 2.2

In ancient times, halite, or rock salt, was so valuable it was "worth its weight in gold." The name comes from the Greek word *hals*, for salt. It sometimes fluoresces red, orange, or green. It is distinguished by how easily it dissolves in water and by its salty taste. **USE:** To preserve and flavor food. **ENVIRONMENT:** Found as a crust around gas vents in volcanic areas; widely distributed in evaporite deposits, formed from the evaporation of closed saltwater basins; found in association with sylvite, gypsum, and anhydrite. **OCCURRENCE:** Salt Lake City, Utah; Death Valley, California; New York; Michigan; New Mexico; Stassfurt, Germany; Galicia, Poland; Chile.

## FLUORITE | CaF — Halide

| | |
|---|---|
| **Crystal System:** Isometric | |
| **Color:** Variable; may be purple, yellow, green, blue, colorless, pink, red, or black | |
| **Transparency:** Transparent to translucent | |
| **Luster:** Glassy | |
| **Streak:** White | |
| **Hardness:** 4.0 | |
| **Habit:** Cubic crystals; granular or columnar; twinning common | |
| **Cleavage:** Perfect in four directions | |
| **Fracture:** Uneven | |
| **Specific Gravity:** 3.2 | |
| **Tests:** Dissolves in sulfuric acid, giving off hydrogen fluoride fumes | |

The name comes from the Latin *fluere*, meaning to flow, referring to its low melting point and its use as a flux in smelting. Fluorite fluoresces under ultraviolet light. Its cubic crystals often have rounded corners. In the past, a color-banded variety known as "blue John" was particularly prized. **USE:** As vases and ornaments—but not jewelry because it is too soft and cleaves too easily; as a flux in the smelting of iron and in the chemical industry; transparent pieces were once used in optical instruments. **ENVIRONMENT:** Found in sedimentary rocks and in pegmatites; widely distributed in veins often in association with metallic ores and quartz, barite, celestite, and dolomite. **OCCURRENCE:** Westmoreland, New Hampshire; Hansonburg district, New Mexico; Clay Center, Ohio; Illinois; Kentucky; Tennessee; Madoc and Faraday Mine in Bancroft, Ontario. Some of the best crystal groups come from Durham and Cumberland, England. Also found in France; Germany; Switzerland; China.

## CALCITE | CaCo₃ — Carbonate

| | |
|---|---|
| **Crystal System:** Hexagonal | |
| **Color:** Usually colorless (Iceland spar) or white; may be gray, yellow, green, purple, or black | |
| **Transparency:** Transparent to translucent; may be almost opaque | |
| **Luster:** Glassy | |
| **Streak:** White | |
| **Hardness:** 3.0 | |
| **Habit:** Tabular, prismatic, or massive/granular; twinning common | |
| **Cleavage:** Perfect in three directions | |
| **Fracture:** Subconchoidal | |
| **Specific Gravity:** 2.7 | |
| **Tests:** Reacts with cold dilute hydrochloric acid to produce effervescence | |

The name comes from the Latin *calx*, for lime. Originally called calcspar. **USE:** Calcite, as limestone, is quarried and used to make cement; as flux in the smelting process; for building or ornamental stone; when flawless and transparent, in polarizing microscopes. **ENVIRONMENT:** One of the most common minerals, calcite forms in all kinds of environments: most often found in limestones and marbles; may be precipitated directly from seawater or formed from shells of marine animals; found in veins with metallic minerals; deposited in caves as stalactites or stalagmites. **OCCURRENCE:** Exceptional crystals come from Joplin, Missouri. Also in Keweenaw Peninsula, Michigan (enclosing copper); Tennessee; Quebec; England; Germany; Mexico; Eskifjord, Iceland (Iceland spar); Namibia; China.

## DOLOMITE | $CaMg(CO_3)_2$                         *Carbonate*

| | |
|---|---|
| **Crystal System:** Hexagonal | |
| **Color:** White, yellow, brown, pink, or (rarely) colorless | |
| **Transparency:** Transparent to translucent | |
| **Luster:** Glassy to pearly | |
| **Streak:** White | |
| **Hardness:** 3.5 to 4.0 | |
| **Habit:** Massive/granular; twinning common | |
| **Cleavage:** Perfect in three directions | |
| **Fracture:** Subconchoidal | |
| **Specific Gravity:** 2.8 to 2.9 | |
| **Tests:** Reacts with warm dilute hydrochloric acid to produce effervescence | |

Dolomite was named for the French scientist Déodat de Dolomieu (1750-1801), who described the mineral on his visit to Egypt with Napoleon Bonaparte in 1798. **USE:** Refractory bricks for furnace linings; dolomitic limestones are used as building stones. **ENVIRONMENT:** A common rock-forming mineral of secondary origin, formed when magnesium-containing solutions interact with limestones; often found in hydrothermal veins with sphalerite and galena. **OCCURRENCE:** Joplin, Missouri; Keokuk, Iowa; Lockport, New York; Colorado; North Carolina; St. Eustache, Quebec; England; Binnenthal, Switzerland; Spain; Guanajuato, Mexico; Brazil.

## MAGNESITE | $MgCO_3$                         *Carbonate*

| | |
|---|---|
| **Crystal System:** Hexagonal | |
| **Color:** White or colorless (pure); may be gray, yellow, or brown (if iron present) | |
| **Transparency:** Transparent to translucent | |
| **Luster:** Glassy | |
| **Streak:** White | |
| **Hardness:** 3.5 to 4.5 | |
| **Habit:** Good crystals rare; prismatic, massive/granular, compact, or fibrous | |
| **Cleavage:** Perfect in three directions | |
| **Fracture:** Conchoidal | |
| **Specific Gravity:** 3.0 to 3.2 (increases with increasing magnesium content) | |
| **Tests:** Effervesces in hot dilute hydrochloric acid | |

The name comes from the Greek *magnesia lithos*, for magnesian stone, an ore of magnesium (Mg) from Magnesia, Thessaly, Greece. **USE:** Cement and refractory bricks. **ENVIRONMENT:** Not as common as calcite or dolomite, it is usually found in veins in magnesium-rich metamorphic rocks such as serpentinites; also formed as a result of interaction of magnesium-containing fluids with carbonate-containing rocks. **OCCURRENCE:** Coast Range, California; Clark County and Paradise Range, Nevada; Oberdorf and Snarum, Austria. Beautiful crystals from Brumado, Bahia, Brazil.

## SIDERITE | $Fe^{+2}CO_3$  *Carbonate*

**Crystal System:** Hexagonal

**Color:** Gray-brown to yellow-brown

**Transparency:** Transparent to translucent

**Luster:** Glassy

**Streak:** White

**Hardness:** 3.5 to 4.5

**Habit:** Massive/granular, fibrous, globular, or earthy; sometimes twinned

**Cleavage:** Perfect in three directions

**Fracture:** Uneven

**Specific Gravity:** 3.8 to 4.0

**Tests:** Dissolves slowly in cold dilute hydrochloric acid; effervesces if acid warmed

The name comes from the Greek *sideros,* for iron. Pseudomorphs of limonite after siderite are common. **USE:** An ore of iron—especially in Europe, but less so in North America. **ENVIRONMENT:** Found in clays and shales as clay ironstone, of concretionary origin; common in hydrothermal veins with metallic ores, including pyrite, chalcopyrite, and galena. **OCCURRENCE:** Roxbury, Connecticut; Vermont; New York; large crystals from Mont St. Hilaire, Quebec; some of best crystals from Cornwall, England; Panasqueria, Portugal; Austria; Germany; Greenland; Brazil.

## RHODOCHROSITE | $MnCO_3$  *Carbonate*

**Crystal System:** Hexagonal

**Color:** Rose to pink; sometimes light gray or brown

**Transparency:** Translucent

**Luster:** Glassy

**Streak:** White

**Hardness:** 3.5 to 4.5

**Habit:** Massive/granular or compact

**Cleavage:** Perfect in three directions

**Fracture:** Uneven

**Specific Gravity:** 3.4 to 3.7

**Tests:** Effervesces in hot dilute hydrochloric acid

The name comes from the Greek *rhodon,* for rose, and *chrosis,* for coloring. When exposed to air, some samples will develop a brown or black crust. **USE:** A minor ore of manganese. **ENVIRONMENT:** Common in hydrothermal veins containing ores of silver, lead, and copper. **OCCURRENCE:** Butte, Montana; Sweet Home Mine, Park County, Colorado; Mont St. Hilaire, Quebec; Sonora, Mexico; Kapnik, Romania; Harz Mountains, Germany; Argentina (as stalactites). Some of the world's best crystal groups come from Hotazel, near Kuruman, South Africa.

## ARAGONITE | $CaCO_3$ — *Carbonate*

**Crystal System:** Orthorhombic

**Color:** Colorless, gray, or white

**Transparency:** Transparent to translucent

**Luster:** Glassy

**Streak:** White

**Hardness:** 3.5 to 4.0

**Habit:** Needlelike, tabular, massive, fibrous, or stalactitic; twinning common

**Cleavage:** Good in one direction; poor in two directions

**Fracture:** Uneven

**Specific Gravity:** 2.9

**Tests:** Effervesces in cold dilute hydrochloric acid

Aragonite is named for the Aragon region in Spain where it was first discovered. Aragonite alters to calcite; many calcite fossil shells were once aragonite. **USE:** None. **ENVIRONMENT:** Occurs in hot-spring deposits; in association with deposits of gypsum; in veins with calcite and dolomite; and in oxidized zone of ore bodies with malachite and smithsonite. **OCCURRENCE:** Beautiful crystals with celestite and sulfur have been found in Wind Cave, Chester County, South Dakota; Sicily; pseudo-hexagonal specimens up to three inches (7.6 cm) across occur in Larimer County, Colorado. Also found in Socorro County, New Mexico; Cumberland, England; Spain; Poland; Tsumeb, Namibia. One special variety, called *flos ferri*, or iron flowers, has been found in New Mexico; Austria; Mexico.

## STRONTIANITE | $SrCO_3$ — *Carbonate*

**Crystal System:** Orthorhombic

**Color:** White, pale green, gray, or pale yellow

**Transparency:** Transparent to translucent

**Luster:** Glassy

**Streak:** White

**Hardness:** 3.5 to 4.0

**Habit:** Prismatic, needlelike, massive/granular, fibrous, or columnar; twinning common

**Cleavage:** Perfect in one direction, poor in one direction

**Fracture:** Uneven

**Specific Gravity:** 3.7

**Tests:** Effervesces in dilute hydrochloric acid

The name comes from Strontian in Scotland, where the mineral was first discovered. **USE:** An ore of strontium; used in the refining of sugar; gives the color red to fireworks and flares. **ENVIRONMENT:** In hydrothermal veins or concretions, often in limestones, associated with celestite, barite, and calcite. **OCCURRENCE:** Known for quality of crystals are Tyrol, Austria; Westphalia, Germany; Strontian, Argyllshire, Scotland. Also found in Strontium Hills, San Bernardino, California; Woodville, Sandusky County, Ohio; Schoharie, New York; Caribou district, British Columbia.

## CERUSSITE | $PbCO_3$ — *Carbonate*

**Crystal System:** Orthorhombic

**Color:** White or gray

**Transparency:** Transparent to translucent

**Luster:** Adamantine

**Streak:** White

**Hardness:** 3.0 to 3.5

**Habit:** Prismatic, tabular, needlelike, or massive/granular; twinning common

**Cleavage:** Good in one direction

**Fracture:** Conchoidal

**Specific Gravity:** 6.4 to 6.6

**Tests:** Effervesces in warm dilute nitric acid

The name comes from the Latin *cerussa*, meaning white lead, an old term used for artificial lead carbonate. **USE:** An important ore of lead. **ENVIRONMENT:** A secondary mineral, it is found in the oxidized zones of lead veins, often in association with galena, smithsonite, pyromorphite, and sphalerite. **OCCURRENCE:** Mammoth Mine, Pinal County, Arizona; Colorado; South Dakota; New Mexico; Leadhills, Lanarkshire, Scotland; Broken Hill, New South Wales, Australia; Ems, Nassau; Morocco; China. Beautiful pseudo-hexagonal twins have been found in Tsumeb, Namibia.

## MALACHITE | $Cu_2^{+2}(CO)_3(OH)_2$ — *Carbonate*

**Crystal System:** Monoclinic

**Color:** Bright to dark green

**Transparency:** Translucent

**Luster:** Silky (fibrous), dull (massive), or adamantine (crystals)

**Streak:** Pale green

**Hardness:** 3.5 to 4.0

**Habit:** Crystals rare; needlelike, prismatic, fibrous, radiating, massive/granular, or globular with bands of varying color; twinning common

**Cleavage:** Perfect in one direction

**Fracture:** Uneven, conchoidal, or splintery

**Specific Gravity:** 3.9 to 4.0

**Tests:** Effervesces in dilute hydrochloric acid

The name comes from the Greek word *moloche*, which means mallow, a flower with lobed leaves. Malachite sometimes pseudomorphs after cuprite. **USE:** An ore of copper; as an ornamental stone to make tabletops and vases, especially in Russia; as a green pigment during the Bronze Age; possibly as kohl, the eye paint used by Ancient Egyptian women. **ENVIRONMENT:** A common secondary mineral occurring in the oxidized zone of copper deposits in association with copper, azurite, and cuprite. **OCCURRENCE:** Bisbee, Arizona; Ducktown, Tennessee; France; Russia; Tsumeb, Namibia; Bwana Mkubwa, Zambia; Zaire; Broken Hill, New South Wales, Australia.

## AZURITE | $Cu_3^{+2}(CO_3)_2(OH)_2$     *Carbonate*

**Crystal System:** Monoclinic

**Color:** Shades of azure-blue

**Transparency:** Transparent to translucent

**Luster:** Glassy

**Streak:** Light blue

**Hardness:** 3.5 to 4.0

**Habit:** Tabular, prismatic, radiating, massive, or earthy

**Cleavage:** Good in two directions

**Fracture:** Conchoidal

**Specific Gravity:** 3.8 to 3.9

**Tests:** Effervesces in nitric or hydrochloric acid

The name is derived from the Persian word *lazhward*, meaning blue. Azurite is often found interbanded with malachite. Pseudomorphs of azurite after malachite are common; less common are pseudomorphs after cuprite. **USE:** A minor ore of copper; one of earliest blue pigments. **ENVIRONMENT:** A secondary mineral occurring in the oxidized zone of copper deposits—not as commonly as malachite—in association with copper, malachite, and cuprite. **OCCURRENCE:** Bisbee and Morenci, Greenlee County, Arizona; New Mexico; California; Chessy, France; Morocco; Mexico; Broken Hill, New South Wales, Australia. Spectacular crystals have been found in Tsumeb, Namibia.

## BORAX | $Na_2B_4O_5(OH)_4•8H_2O$     *Borate*

**Crystal System:** Monoclinic

**Color:** Colorless to white; sometimes gray

**Transparency:** Translucent

**Luster:** Glassy to resinous; sometimes dull

**Streak:** White

**Hardness:** 2.0 to 2.5

**Habit:** Prismatic or massive

**Cleavage:** Perfect in one direction; good in one direction

**Fracture:** Conchoidal

**Specific Gravity:** 1.7

The name is derived from the Persian *buraq*, for white. **USE:** As a cleansing material; as a solvent in various smelting and laboratory procedures. **ENVIRONMENT:** The most common of the borate minerals; formed by the evaporation of saline water, in association with other evaporites such as halite. **OCCURRENCE:** In layers up to ten feet (3 m) thick at Boron, Kramer, Kern County, Borax Lake, Lake County, California; Nevada; New Mexico; Tibet; India; Afghanistan.

## COLEMANITE | $Ca_2B_6O_{11} \cdot 5H_2O$      *Borate*

**Crystal System:** Monoclinic

**Color:** Colorless to white; sometimes gray

**Transparency:** Transparent to translucent

**Luster:** Glassy

**Streak:** White

**Hardness:** 4.0 to 4.5

**Habit:** Prismatic, compact, or massive/granular

**Cleavage:** Perfect in one direction; distinct in one direction

**Fracture:** Uneven

**Specific Gravity:** 2.4

The mineral owes its name to William Tell Coleman, a nineteenth-century American mine owner who was instrumental in the founding of the California borax industry. **USE:** A source of borax. **ENVIRONMENT:** As a secondary mineral precipitated from borate-rich water in sedimentary rocks cavities. **OCCURRENCE:** Death Valley, Inyo, and Kern counties, California; Argentina. Beautiful large crystals have been found near Eskisehir, Turkey.

## APATITE GROUP | $Ca_5(PO_4)_3(F, Cl, OH)_3$      *Phosphate*

**Crystal System:** Hexagonal

**Color:** Green, gray-green, red, blue, brown, or (rarely) white

**Transparency:** Transparent to translucent

**Luster:** Glassy

**Streak:** White

**Hardness:** 5.0

**Habit:** Prismatic (barrel-shaped), tabular, globular, or massive/granular

**Cleavage:** Poor in one direction

**Fracture:** Conchoidal or uneven

**Specific Gravity:** 3.1 to 3.3

The name comes from the Greek *apatan*, meaning to deceive—apatite is easily confused with minerals of similar appearance. Once believed to be a single mineral, it is now known to be several, the most common ones being fluorapatite, chloroapatite, and hydroxylapatite. Chemical testing is usually needed to tell them apart. General reference to apatite usually means fluorapatite. **USE:** As fertilizer because of its high phosphorus content; despite its softness, transparent specimens are sometimes used as gemstones. **ENVIRONMENT:** As an accessory mineral in almost all igneous rocks; in metamorphic rocks; in veins associated with ore deposits; and as the chief mineral in phosphate rocks. **OCCURRENCE:** Large deep-blue crystals found in Hugo Mine, Keystone, South Dakota. Also found in New York; California; Maine; Ontario; Quebec; Spain; Portugal; Germany; Austria; Italy; Bolivia.

## MIMETITE | $Pb_5(AsO_4)_3Cl$ — *Arsenate*

| | |
|---|---|
| **Crystal System:** Hexagonal | |
| **Color:** Pale yellow to yellow-brown | |
| **Transparency:** Subtransparent to translucent | |
| **Luster:** Resinous | |
| **Streak:** White | |
| **Hardness:** 3.5 to 4.0 | |
| **Habit:** Prismatic, needlelike, or globular | |
| **Cleavage:** Poor | |
| **Fracture:** Uneven | |
| **Specific Gravity:** 7.0 to 7.2 | |

The name comes from the Greek *mimetus*, meaning imitator, because of its resemblance to pyromorphite (chemical testing is often needed to distinguish them). **USE:** A minor lead ore. **ENVIRONMENT:** Relatively rare; usually found as an accessory mineral in oxidized zone of lead veins, especially those containing arsenic. **OCCURRENCE:** California; Pennsylvania; Colorado; Leadhills, Scotland; Cornwall and Cumberland, England; Tsumeb, Namibia. Beautiful specimens occur in Mapimi, Durango, Mexico.

## ADAMITE | $Zn_2(AsO_4)(OH)$ — *Arsenate*

| | |
|---|---|
| **Crystal System:** Orthorhombic | |
| **Color:** Yellow to green; sometimes violet, reddish brown, or (rarely) turquoise | |
| **Transparency:** Transparent to translucent | |
| **Luster:** Glassy | |
| **Streak:** White or green | |
| **Hardness:** 3.5 | |
| **Habit:** Crystals usually small; commonly radiating aggregates | |
| **Cleavage:** Good in one direction; poor in one direction | |
| **Fracture:** Uneven | |
| **Specific Gravity:** 4.3 to 4.4 | |

Adamite was discovered at Chanarcillo, Chile, by Gilbert-Joseph Adam, a nineteenth-century French mineralogist and author of the celebrated *Tableau minéralogigue* (1869). **USE:** None. **ENVIRONMENT:** A rare secondary mineral found in oxidized zone of zinc sulfide deposits. **OCCURRENCE:** Golden Hill Mine, Toole County, Utah; Inyo and San Bernardino counties, California; Mapimi, Durango, Mexico; Tsumeb, Namibia, and Laurium, Greece.

## VANADINITE | $Pb_5(VO_4)_3Cl$ — *Vanadate*

| | |
|---|---|
| **Crystal System:** Hexagonal | |
| **Color:** Orange-red; brown-red to yellow. | |
| **Transparency:** Transparent to translucent | |
| **Luster:** Resinous | |
| **Streak:** White to yellowish | |
| **Hardness:** 3.0 | |
| **Habit:** Prismatic, fibrous, compact, or globular | |
| **Cleavage:** N/A | |
| **Fracture:** Uneven; conchoidal | |
| **Specific Gravity:** 6.7 to 7.1 | |

The name vanadinite was given to the mineral to reflect its vanadium (element) content. Some of the dark red and orange specimens lose their color with exposure to light. **USE:** An ore of vanadium; a minor ore of lead. **ENVIRONMENT:** A relatively rare secondary mineral found in oxidized zone of lead sulfide deposits. **OCCURRENCE:** Mammoth Mine in Pinal County, Apache Mine in Gila County, Arizona; Chihuahua, Mexico. Some of best specimens come from Mibladen, Morocco.

## WAVELLITE | $Al_3(PO_4)_2(OH,F)_3 \cdot 5H_2O$ — *Phosphate*

| | |
|---|---|
| **Crystal System:** Orthorhombic | |
| **Color:** White, green, yellow, gray, or brown | |
| **Transparency:** Translucent | |
| **Luster:** Glassy | |
| **Streak:** White | |
| **Hardness:** 3.5 to 4.0 | |
| **Habit:** Radiating aggregates in spheres, prismatic, or striated; also forms crusts | |
| **Cleavage:** Perfect in one direction; good in two directions | |
| **Fracture:** Uneven; conchoidal | |
| **Specific Gravity:** 2.3 to 2.4 | |

Wavellite is named for William Wavell (d. 1829), the English physician who discovered it. It has also been called fischerite. **USE:** None. **ENVIRONMENT:** A secondary mineral often found on joint surfaces or in cavities in rocks, especially slates; also found in association with phosphorite deposits. **OCCURRENCE:** Garland, Hot Spring, Arkansas; St. Clair County, Alabama; England; France; Portugal; Bolivia.

## VARISCITE | $AlPO_4 \cdot 2H_2O$     *Phosphate*

**Crystal System:**
Orthorhombic

**Color:** Light to emerald green, blue, or (rarely) colorless

**Transparency:** Transparent to translucent

**Luster:** Waxy to dull (massive); glassy (crystals)

**Streak:** White

**Hardness:** 3.5 to 4.5

**Habit:** Crystals rare; massive, crusts, nodules, or veins

**Cleavage:** N/A

**Fracture:** Uneven (massive); conchoidal (crystals)

**Specific Gravity:** 2.2 to 2.8

Variscite is named after the location where it was discovered: Variscia, the old name for the Voightland district in Saxony, Germany. **USE:** In jewelry, in cabochon cut as a substitute for turquoise. **ENVIRONMENT:** A secondary mineral formed when phosphorous-containing waters interact with aluminum-rich rocks. **OCCURRENCE:** Arkansas; California; Fairfield, Utah County, Utah; Germany; Austria; Brazil; Australia.

## TURQUOISE | $Cu^{+2}Al_6(PO_4)_4(OH)_8 \cdot 4H_2O$     *Phosphate*

**Crystal System:** Triclinic

**Color:** Sky-blue, blue-green, or greenish gray

**Transparency:** Subtranslucent to opaque

**Luster:** Waxy (massive); glassy (crystals)

**Streak:** White or greenish

**Hardness:** 5.0 to 6.0

**Habit:** Crystals rare; massive, globular, or veins

**Cleavage:** N/A

**Fracture:** Conchoidal

**Specific Gravity:** 2.6 to 2.8

The name turquoise comes from the French word *turquoise*, meaning Turkish, because the stone found its way to Europe through Turkey from the southern slopes of the Al-Mirsah-Kuh Mountains, near Nishapur, Iran. **USE:** Considered to be a semiprecious gem, it is always used as a cabochon stone, never faceted. **ENVIRONMENT:** A secondary mineral found in veins in association with weathered aluminum-rich igneous or sedimentary rocks in arid regions. **OCCURRENCE:** New Mexico; Arizona; California; Lynch Station, Campbell County, Virginia; France; Chile; Egypt; Iran; China.

## AUTUNITE | $Ca(UO_2)_2(PO_4)_2 \cdot 10–12H_2O$      *Phosphate*

**Crystal System:** Tetragonal

**Color:** Lemon-yellow to greenish yellow

**Transparency:** Subadamantine

**Luster:** Glassy; pearly parallel to cleavage

**Streak:** Yellow

**Hardness:** 2.0 to 2.5

**Habit:** Tabular, foliated, scaly, or platy

**Cleavage:** Perfect in one direction

**Fracture:** N/A

**Specific Gravity:** 3.2

Autunite is named for its discovery location, Autun, Saône-et-Loire, France. **USE:** An ore of uranium, prized by collectors for its color. Chemical testing is needed in order to distinguish it from some of the other secondary uranium minerals. **ENVIRONMENT:** A secondary mineral that occurs in the oxidized zones of veins and pegmatites that contain uranium minerals. **OCCURRENCE:** Daybreak Mine, Mt. Spokane, Washington; Keystone and Custer districts, South Dakota; Colorado; Utah; California; Autun, Saône-et-Loire, France; Saxony, Germany; St. Austel and Redruth, Cornwall, England; Rum Jungle area, Northern Territory, Australia.

## BARITE | $BaSO_4$      *Sulfate*

**Crystal System:** Orthorhombic

**Color:** Colorless to white, yellow, brown, blue, green, or red

**Transparency:** Transparent to translucent

**Luster:** Glassy

**Streak:** White

**Hardness:** 3.0 to 3.5

**Habit:** Tabular, prismatic, fibrous, scaly, granular, or stalactitic

**Cleavage:** Perfect in one direction; good in one direction; distinct in one direction

**Fracture:** Uneven

**Specific Gravity:** 4.3 to 4.6

The name comes from the Greek word *barys*, meaning heavy. Barite sometimes forms radially symmetrical groups of crystals, called desert roses, in sands, soft sandstones, and clays. **USE:** Most common mineral of barium; used in oil- and gas-well drilling. **ENVIRONMENT:** In sedimentary rocks, in veins, and as a gangue mineral with sulfide ores and calcite, quartz, fluorite, and siderite. **OCCURRENCE:** Fall River, Meade, South Dakota; blue crystals near Stoneham, Weld County, Colorado; desert roses near Norman, Oklahoma; beautiful crystals from Cumberland, Northumberland, and Westmoreland, England. Also found in Germany; France; Spain.

## CELESTITE | $SrSO_4$                                    *Sulfate*

**Crystal System:** Orthorhombic

**Color:** Colorless to pale blue-white; sometimes reddish

**Transparency:** Transparent to translucent

**Luster:** Glassy

**Streak:** White

**Hardness:** 3.0 to 3.5

**Habit:** Prismatic, tabular, fibrous, or granular

**Cleavage:** Perfect in one direction; good in one direction; distinct in one direction

**Fracture:** Uneven

**Specific Gravity:** 3.9 to 4.0

The name comes from the Latin word *caelestis*, for sky—celestite often displays a light blue tint on its white or colorless crystals. **USE:** In a preparation of nitrate of strontium for fireworks. **ENVIRONMENT:** Found in sedimentary rocks, particularly in sandstones or limestones, in association with barite, gypsum, halite, calcite, and fluorite. **OCCURRENCE:** Ohio; Texas; West Virginia; Canada. Superb crystal groups associated with aragonite and sulphur in Sicily, Italy. Also found in England; France; Switzerland; Madagascar; Mexico; Egypt.

## ANHYDRITE | $CaSO_4$                                    *Sulfate*

**Crystal System:** Orthorhombic

**Color:** Colorless to white, often with bluish tinge

**Transparency:** Transparent to translucent

**Luster:** Glassy to pearly

**Streak:** White

**Hardness:** 3.0 to 3.5

**Habit:** Crystals rare; usually massive/granular or fibrous

**Cleavage:** Good in three directions at ninety degrees

**Fracture:** Uneven

**Specific Gravity:** 2.9 to 3.0

This mineral contains no water; its name comes from the Greek words, *an*, for without, and *hydro*, for water. It is a relatively rare mineral, possibly because when it absorbs water it becomes gypsum. For example, large anhydrite beds in Nova Scotia are now mostly gypsum. **USE:** None. **ENVIRONMENT:** An evaporite mineral deposited from seawater; in the cap rock above salt domes; and in minor amounts in sulfide ore veins. **OCCURRENCE:** Carlsbad, New Mexico; Ajo, Arizona; Massachusetts; New York; Nova Scotia; Faraday Uranium Mine, Bancroft, Ontario; Germany; Poland; France; Switzerland; Mexico; India.

## CROCOITE | PbCrO$_4$          *Chromate*

| | |
|---|---|
| **Crystal System:** Monoclinic | |
| **Color:** Orange-red to brown | |
| **Transparency:** Translucent | |
| **Luster:** Adamantine to glassy | |
| **Streak:** Orange-yellow | |
| **Hardness:** 2.5 to 3.0 | |
| **Habit:** Prismatic, needlelike, massive/granular, striated lengthwise, or columnar | |
| **Cleavage:** Distinct in one direction; poor in two directions | |
| **Fracture:** Uneven | |
| **Specific Gravity:** 5.9 to 6.1 | |

The name crocoite comes from the Greek word *krokos*, for saffron, because of its color. The element chromium (Cr) was first discovered in crocoite. **USE:** None. **ENVIRONMENT:** As a rare secondary mineral in oxidized zone of lead ores, often in association with pyromorphite, mimetite, and cerussite. **OCCURRENCE:** Darwin Mine in Inyo County, El Dorado Mine in Riverside County, California; Mammoth Mine, Pinal County, Arizona; Russia; Minas Gerais, Brazil. The world's best known specimens come from Tasmania.

## GYPSUM | CaSO$_4$·2H$_2$O          *Sulfate*

| | |
|---|---|
| **Crystal System:** Monoclinic | |
| **Color:** Colorless to white; may be yellow, gray, red, or brown | |
| **Transparency:** Transparent to translucent | |
| **Luster:** Glassy or silky; pearly parallel to cleavage | |
| **Streak:** White | |
| **Hardness:** 2.0 | |
| **Habit:** Crystals tabular, often with curved faces; fibrous or massive/granular; twinning common | |
| **Cleavage:** Perfect in one direction; good in two directions | |
| **Fracture:** Conchoidal; splintery | |
| **Specific Gravity:** 2.3 | |

Gypsum comes in a number of visually distinct varieties. Selenite is colorless and transparent; satin spar is white, fibrous, and silky in luster; alabaster is fine-grained. **USE:** As plaster—its name comes from the Greek word *gypos*, for chalk. **ENVIRONMENT:** Found in massive evaporite deposits, often in association with halite and anhydrite; in smaller amounts in volcanic areas; as free crystals in clay; and in mineral veins where pyrite has oxidized and reacted with calcareous rock. **OCCURRENCE:** California; Pennsylvania; Colorado; Oklahoma; South Dakota; New Mexico; Nova Scotia; France; Poland; Austria. Crystals up to ten feet (3 m) in length have been found at Braden Mine, Chile. The Cave of Swords at Naica, Chihuahua, Mexico, is famous for its three- to five-foot (1- to 1.5-m)-long slender needles of gypsum containing bubbles of water.

## WOLFRAMITE | (Fe,Mn)WO₄ — $(Fe,Mn)WO_4$ — *Tungstate*

| | |
|---|---|
| **Crystal System:** | Monoclinic |
| **Color:** | Gray-black to brown-black |
| **Transparency:** | Opaque |
| **Luster:** | Submetallic |
| **Streak:** | Brownish black |
| **Hardness:** | 4.0 to 4.5 |
| **Habit:** | Tabular, prismatic, or massive/granular |
| **Cleavage:** | Perfect in one direction lengthwise |
| **Fracture:** | Uneven |
| **Specific Gravity:** | 7.0 to 7.5 |

Wolframite is an intermediary species in the series between ferberite ($FeWO_4$) and hübnerite ($MnWO_4$). Sometimes wolframite alters to scheelite. **USE:** An ore of tungsten. **ENVIRONMENT:** Found in quartz veins and pegmatites associated with granites, often with cassiterite, arsenopyrite, tourmaline, scheelite, galena, and sphalerite; also as a placer deposit. **OCCURRENCE:** Laos County, New Mexico; Black Hills, South Dakota; Canada; Germany. Beautiful specimens found in Schlaggenwald and Zinnwald, Bohemia, Czechoslovakia. Also found in Bolivia; Argentina; Iran; China.

## SCHEELITE | CaWO₄ — $CaWO_4$ — *Tungstate*

| | |
|---|---|
| **Crystal System:** | Tetragonal |
| **Color:** | White, light brown, or light green |
| **Transparency:** | Transparent to translucent |
| **Luster:** | Glassy |
| **Streak:** | White |
| **Hardness:** | 4.5 to 5.0 |
| **Habit:** | Crystals bipyramidal; massive/granular; twinning common |
| **Cleavage:** | Distinct in one direction; poor in two directions |
| **Fracture:** | Uneven |
| **Specific Gravity:** | 5.9 to 6.1 |

Scheelite was named for Karl Wilhelm Scheele, an eighteenth-century Swedish chemist who proved the existence of tungstic oxide in the mineral. Scheelite is often fluorescent, blue to yellow, depending on its molybdenum content. **USE:** An ore of tungsten; used for tools and in the aerospace industry. **ENVIRONMENT:** Found in pegmatites and hydrothermal veins in association with wolframite, molybdenite, fluorite, and topaz. **OCCURRENCE:** Trumbull, Fairfield County, Connecticut; Custer, Lawrence County, South Dakota; Darwin, Inyo County, California; Cochise and Mojave counties, Arizona; Canada; Germany; Switzerland; Italy; Mexico; Brazil; Peru; Australia. Beautiful large crystals from Japan; Korea; China.

## WULFENITE | $PbMoO_4$      *Molybdate*

**Crystal System:** Tetragonal

**Color:** Orange-yellow, orange, brown, gray, green-brown, or tan

**Transparency:** Transparent to translucent

**Luster:** Resinous to adamantine

**Streak:** White

**Hardness:** 2.75 to 3.0

**Habit:** Platy, prismatic, or massive/granular

**Cleavage:** Distinct in one direction

**Fracture:** Uneven

**Specific Gravity:** 6.5 to 7.0

Wulfenite is named for Franz Xavier Wülfen, an eighteenth-century Jesuit mineralogist who wrote about the lead ores at the mineral's discovery site in Bleiberg, Carinthia, Austria.
**USE:** A minor ore of molybdenum. **ENVIRONMENT:** A secondary mineral formed in oxidized zones of lead and molybdenum ores. **OCCURRENCE:** Wheatley Mine, Chester County, Pennsylvania; Glove Mine, Red Cloud Mine, and Mammoth Mine, Arizona; New Mexico; Utah; South Dakota; California; Bleiberg, Austria; Germany; Mexico; Australia; Morocco; Tsumeb, Namibia.

## OLIVINE GROUP | $(Mg,Fe^{+2})_2SiO_4$      *Silicate*

**Crystal System:** Orthorhombic

**Color:** Olive-green, yellow, light gray, or brown; may appear reddish (oxidized)

**Transparency:** Transparent to translucent

**Luster:** Glassy

**Streak:** White

**Hardness:** 6.5 to 7.0

**Habit:** Massive/granular

**Cleavage:** Indistinct in two directions at ninety degrees

**Fracture:** Conchoidal

**Specific Gravity:** 3.3 to 4.4 (increases with increasing iron content)

Olivine is an intermediary species in the series between forsterite ($Mg_2SiO_4$) and fayalite ($Fe^{+2}SiO_4$). The name refers to the common olive-green color of the magnesium variety. **USE:** As a gemstone (peridot, the clear, green variety). **ENVIRONMENT:** A rock-forming mineral in rocks low in silica, such as basalt and gabbro; in metamorphosed iron-rich sediments and dolomitic limestones; the rock dunite is composed entirely of olivine; since it is never found with free quartz, it is never found in granite. **OCCURRENCE:** Yellowstone Park, Wyoming; Rockport, Massachusetts; New Mexico; Arizona; Hawaii; California; Greenland; Sweden; France; Germany; Finland. Main source of peridots is St. John's Island, Red Sea.

## GARNET GROUP | $X_3Y_2(SiO_4)_3$ — *Silicate*

**Crystal System:** Isometric

**Color:** Variable; depends on composition

**Transparency:** Transparent to translucent

**Luster:** Glassy

**Streak:** White

**Hardness:** 6.0 to 7.5

**Habit:** Crystals common; dodecahedral; massive/granular

**Cleavage:** N/A

**Fracture:** Uneven

**Specific Gravity:** 3.5 to 4.3

*Spessartine*

*Grossular*

Garnets represent a group of minerals composed of aluminum silicates (pyrope-almandine-spessartine series) and calcium silicates (andradite-grossular-uvavorite series). Most red garnets used in jewelry today are pyrope or almandine. **USE:** Ground garnets are used as abrasives; many garnets are considered semi-precious gemstones, including rhodolite (rose or purple member of pyrope-almandine series), hessonite (yellow grossular), and demantoid (green andradite). **ENVIRONMENT:** Some garnets are found in igneous rocks—such as pyrope, which is found in peridotites, serpentinites, and kimberlites; others, such as almandine, spessartine, andradite, and grossular, are found in metamorphic rocks. Various kinds are found as alluvial deposits in beach and river sands. **OCCURRENCE:** Macon County, North Carolina; Minot, Maine; Warren, New Hampshire; Salida, Chaffee County, Colorado; Connecticut; California; Arizona; Alaska; Quebec; Italy; Switzerland; Sweden; Norway; Greenland; Russia; Mexico; Australia.

## ZIRCON | $ZrSiO_4$ — *Silicate*

**Crystal System:** Tetragonal

**Color:** Brown, colorless, gray, green, reddish, bluish, or violet

**Transparency:** Transparent to translucent

**Luster:** Adamantine

**Streak:** Colorless

**Hardness:** 6.5 to 7.5

**Habit:** Prismatic or granular; twinning rare

**Cleavage:** Indistinct in two directions

**Fracture:** Conchoidal

**Specific Gravity:** 4.0 to 4.7

The name comes from the Persian *azargun—azar*, meaning gold, and *gun*, meaning colored; zircon sometimes appears gold. Zircon commonly fluoresces yellow-orange. **USE:** As gemstones (transparent zircons); as a source for zirconium oxide, the most refractory substance known, used to make cubic zirconia, one of the better diamond substitutes; as a source for metallic zirconium, used in the production of nuclear reactors. **ENVIRONMENT:** Widely distributed in sedimentary rock, in hydrothermal veins where it is found in association with minerals such as sphalerite, pyrite, chalcopyrite, quartz, dolomite, barite, and fluorite; less often in pegmatites. **OCCURRENCE:** St. Peter's Dome, El Paso County, Colorado; Llano County, Texas; Tin Mountain, Custer County, South Dakota; Quebec; Ontario; France; Italy; Germany; Brazil; Korea; Australia.

## ANDALUSITE | $Al_2SiO_5$                                    *Silicate*

**Crystal System:**
Orthorhombic

**Color:** Pink, red, gray, brown, or green

**Transparency:** Transparent to nearly opaque

**Luster:** Glassy

**Streak:** Colorless

**Hardness:** 6.5 to 7.5

**Habit:** Columnar, granular, or prismatic with square cross-section; some crystals contain dark carbonaceous inclusions, which in cross-section form a dark cross (chiastolites)

**Cleavage:** Good in two directions at eighty-nine degrees

**Fracture:** Uneven

**Specific Gravity:** 3.1 to 3.2

Andalusite is named after the location where it was discovered, the Andalusia region in Spain. It sometimes alters to a white mica, which can be found coating the crystals. **USE:** The manufacture of spark plugs and other porcelains of a high refractory nature; as gemstones (transparent green variety only). **ENVIRONMENT:** Found in schists, slates, gneisses, and alluvial deposits; in association with corundum, tourmaline, topaz, sillimanite, and kyanite. **OCCURRENCE:** Inyo Range, Mono County, California; Black Hills, South Dakota; Colorado; New Mexico; Maine; Massachusetts; Sweden; France; Germany; Spain; Brazil; Korea; Australia.

## KYANITE | $Al_2SiO_5$                                    *Silicate*

**Crystal System:** Triclinic

**Color:** Blue to white; may be green or gray

**Transparency:** Transparent to translucent

**Luster:** Glassy; pearly on cleavage surfaces

**Streak:** Colorless

**Hardness:** 4.0 to 5.0 (along prism) and 7.0 (across)

**Habit:** Bladed; radiating bladed

**Cleavage:** Perfect in one direction lengthwise, good in one direction

**Fracture:** Splintery

**Specific Gravity:** 3.6 to 3.7

The name comes from the Greek word *kyanos*, for blue, referring to kyanite's most common color. Sometimes the crystals are unevenly colored in splotches or streaks, with the darkest color occurring at the center of the crystals. **USE:** Used in the manufacture of spark plugs and other porcelains of a high refractory nature. **ENVIRONMENT:** Found in regionally metamorphosed schists and gneisses, and associated pegmatites and quartz veins; in association with garnet, staurolite, mica, and quartz. **OCCURRENCE:** California; Idaho; Georgia; Canada; Ireland; France; Italy; St. Gothard, Switzerland; India; Brazil; Korea; Australia.

## TOPAZ | $Al_2SiO_4(F,OH)_2$

*Silicate*

**Crystal System:** Orthorhombic

**Color:** Colorless, white, pale blue, light yellow, yellow-brown, pink-brown, or pink

**Transparency:** Transparent to translucent

**Luster:** Glassy

**Streak:** Colorless

**Hardness:** 8.0

**Habit:** Prismatic or massive/granular

**Cleavage:** Perfect in one direction

**Fracture:** Conchoidal

**Specific Gravity:** 3.5 to 3.6

The name comes from the Greek *topazion*, which may derive from the Sanskrit *tapas*, for fire, or from Topazios, the Greek name for the Island of Zabargad in the Red Sea. Topaz crystals up to several hundred pounds have been found. Pink gem topaz is obtained by heat treating dark yellow stones. **USE:** Clear or finely colored varieties used as gems; deep gold-yellow type most prized. Sometimes brown quartz is falsely sold as topaz. **ENVIRONMENT:** Found in veins and cavities in pegmatites and other igneous rocks, in association with fluorite, tourmaline, apatite, beryl, and cassiterite; also found in alluvial deposits. **OCCURRENCE:** San Diego County, California; Thomas Mountain, Juab County, Utah; Pike's Peak region, Colorado; Texas; Lords Hill, Maine; Ireland; Norway; Sweden; Germany; Russia; Pakistan; Mexico; Brazil; Nigeria; Japan; Australia.

## STAUROLITE | $(Fe^{+2},Mg,Zn)_2Al_9(Si,Al)_4O_{22}(OH)_2$

*Silicate*

**Crystal System:** Monoclinic or pseudo-orthorhombic

**Color:** Reddish to dark brown

**Transparency:** Translucent to almost opaque

**Luster:** Glassy to resinous

**Streak:** White

**Hardness:** 7.0 to 7.5

**Habit:** Prismatic; rarely massive; twinning common

**Cleavage:** Distinct in one direction

**Fracture:** Uneven

**Specific Gravity:** 3.6 to 3.7

The name comes from the Greek *stauros*, meaning a cross, referring to the common cruciform twin habit of the mineral. **USE:** Rare transparent stones from Brazil have been cut as gems. **ENVIRONMENT:** Usually found as individual or twinned crystals in medium-grade schists and gneisses, in association with garnet, kyanite, and mica. **OCCURRENCE:** Rio Arriba County, New Mexico; Black Hills, South Dakota; Fannin County, Georgia; Maine; Virginia; Canada; Greenland; Ireland; Scotland; France; Switzerland; Brazil.

## CHONDRODITE | $(Mg,Fe^{+2})_5(SiO_4)_2(F,OH)_2$ — *Silicate*

**Crystal System:** Monoclinic

**Color:** Red-brown to yellow

**Transparency:** Transparent to translucent

**Luster:** Glassy

**Streak:** Colorless

**Hardness:** 6.0-6.5

**Habit:** Stubby crystals; massive/granular; twinning common

**Cleavage:** Poor in one direction

**Fracture:** Uneven

**Specific Gravity:** 3.1 to 3.2

The name comes from the Greek word *chondros*, meaning grain, because chondrodite often is granular in appearance. Sometimes chondrodite fluoresces yellow. **USE:** None. **ENVIRONMENT:** In metamorphosed limestones or dolomites, in association with spinel, phlogopite, garnet, vesuvianite, diopside, graphite, and calcite. **OCCURRENCE:** Riverside and San Bernardino counties, California; Tilly Foster Iron Mine, Brewster, Putnam County, New York; Cardiff Uranium Mine, Wilberforce, Ontario; Sweden; Finland; Mount Vesuvius, Campania, Italy.

## TITANITE | $CaTiSiO_5$ — *Silicate*

**Crystal System:** Monoclinic

**Color:** Brown or greenish yellow; sometimes gray or nearly black

**Transparency:** Transparent to translucent, sometimes almost opaque

**Luster:** Adamantine to resinous

**Streak:** White

**Hardness:** 5.0 to 5.5

**Habit:** Tabular, scaly, or massive; twinning common

**Cleavage:** Distinct in two directions

**Fracture:** Conchoidal

**Specific Gravity:** 3.4 to 3.5

Titanite was (and sometimes still is) known as sphene, which comes from the Greek *sphen*, meaning wedge, a reference to the common crystal habit; the name titanite reflects its titanium content. **USE:** A source of titanium. **ENVIRONMENT:** As an accessory mineral in igneous and metamorphic rocks, including syenite, diorite, schists, and gneisses. **OCCURRENCE:** Riverside County, California; Magnet Cove, Arkansas; Franklin, New Jersey; Butte, Montana. The best North American specimens come from Renfrew, Ontario. Also found in St. Gothard, Switzerland; Kola Peninsula, Russia; Minas Gerais, Brazil.

## NEPTUNITE | $KNa_2Li(Fe^{+2},Mn^{+2})_2Ti_2Si_8O_{24}$     *Silicate*

| | |
|---|---|
| **Crystal System:** Monoclinic | |
| **Color:** Black with reddish reflections | |
| **Transparency:** Nearly opaque, translucent on thin edges | |
| **Luster:** Glassy | |
| **Streak:** Reddish brown | |
| **Hardness:** 5.0 to 6.0 | |
| **Habit:** Prismatic, often with square cross-section | |
| **Cleavage:** Perfect in one direction lengthwise; good in two directions | |
| **Fracture:** Conchoidal | |
| **Specific Gravity:** 3.2 | |

Neptunite was named for Neptune, Roman god of the sea, because it was found with the mineral aegerine, named after Aegir, the Scandinavian sea god. The mineral forms a series with mangan-neptunite. **USE:** None. **ENVIRONMENT:** A rare mineral found in cavities in nepheline syenites and in serpentine veins, in association with the minerals natrolite, benitoite, and joaquinite. **OCCURRENCE:** Beautiful crystals occur with benitoite near the headwaters of San Benito River, San Benito County, California. Also found in Narsarussak, Greenland; Kola Peninsula, Russia.

## DIOPTASE | $Cu^{+2}SiO_2(OH)_2$     *Silicate*

| | |
|---|---|
| **Crystal System:** Hexagonal | |
| **Color:** Emerald-green | |
| **Transparency:** Transparent to translucent | |
| **Luster:** Glassy | |
| **Streak:** Pale green-blue | |
| **Hardness:** 5.0 | |
| **Habit:** Prismatic or massive/granular | |
| **Cleavage:** Perfect in three directions | |
| **Fracture:** Uneven to conchoidal | |
| **Specific Gravity:** 3.3 to 3.4 | |

The name comes from the Greek *dia*, for through, and *optasia*, for vision, because cleavage planes are visible in transparent crystals. **USE:** None. **ENVIRONMENT:** An uncommon mineral found in the oxidized zone of copper deposits, especially in arid climates. **OCCURRENCE:** Soda Lake Mountains, San Bernardino, California; Mammoth Mine, Arizona; Russia; Copiapo, Atacama, Chile. Some of world's best dioptase found in Tsumeb, Namibia.

## EPIDOTE | $Ca_2(Fe^{+3},Al)_3(SiO_4)_3(OH)$      *Silicate*

| | |
|---|---|
| **Crystal System:** Monoclinic | |
| **Color:** Pistachio-green, green, or blackish green | |
| **Transparency:** Transparent to translucent | |
| **Luster:** Glassy; may be pearly on cleavage surfaces | |
| **Streak:** Colorless to gray | |
| **Hardness:** 6.0 to 7.0 | |
| **Habit:** Prismatic, often striated, tabular, massive/granular, or fibrous; twinning rare | |
| **Cleavage:** Perfect in one direction | |
| **Fracture:** Uneven | |
| **Specific Gravity:** 3.4 to 3.5 | |

The name epidote may come from the Greek *epidosis*, meaning increase, referring to the fact that one side of its crystal is longer than the other. When rotated, translucent prisms of epidote display strong dichroism—the color is dark green in one direction and brown in another. **USE:** None. **ENVIRONMENT:** Widespread in low-grade metamorphic rocks derived from granites, diabases, or calcareous sediments. **OCCURRENCE:** Sulzer, Prince of Wales Island, Alaska; Adams County, Idaho; Calumet Iron Mine, Chaffee County, and Epidote Hill, Park County, Colorado; Baja California, Mexico; Switzerland; Austria; Pakistan. Attractive crystals found in Bourg d'Oissans, France.

## VESUVIANITE | $Ca_{10}Mg_2Al_4(SiO_4)_5(Si_2O_7)_2(OH)_4$      *Silicate*

| | |
|---|---|
| **Crystal System:** Tetragonal | |
| **Color:** Usually dark green or brown; also yellow, blue (cyprine), or violet | |
| **Transparency:** Transparent to translucent | |
| **Luster:** Glassy | |
| **Streak:** White | |
| **Hardness:** 6.5 | |
| **Habit:** Prismatic, often striated parallel to length, massive, granular, or columnar | |
| **Cleavage:** Poor in one direction | |
| **Fracture:** Uneven | |
| **Specific Gravity:** 3.4 to 3.5 | |

This mineral is named after the volcanic blocks ejected from Mount Vesuvius in Campania, Italy, where it was first discovered. It was (and often still is) called idocrase. **USE:** None. **ENVIRONMENT:** Found in metamorphosed limestones in association with grossular, wollastonite, diopside, and calcite. **OCCURRENCE:** Franconia, New Hampshire; Roxbury, Connecticut; Franklin, New Jersey; Deloro, Ontario. Attractive purple and green crystal groups found in Thetford, Quebec. Also found in England; Norway; France; Japan.

## BERYL | $Be_3Al_2Si_6O_{18}$

*Silicate*

**Crystal System:** Hexagonal

**Color:** White, blue, yellow, green, or pink

**Transparency:** Transparent to translucent

**Luster:** Glassy

**Streak:** Colorless

**Hardness:** 7.5 to 8.0

**Habit:** Prismatic, often striated parallel to length, or massive

**Cleavage:** Indistinct in one direction

**Fracture:** Uneven to conchoidal

**Specific Gravity:** 2.6 to 2.8

*Emerald*

The name beryl comes from the Greek *beryllos*, meaning blue-green gem. Also known as the fortune-teller's jewel. Beryl's various color varieties have been given their own names: dark or light green (emerald), blue-green (aquamarine), yellow (heliodor), and pink (morganite). Some emeralds fluoresce pink to deep red. **USE:** As a source for beryllium; as a gemstone, both precious

*Morganite*

and semiprecious. **ENVIRONMENT:** Found as an accessory mineral in granites and granite pegmatites; also in mica schists. **OCCURRENCE:** Joplin, Missouri; Colorado; Utah; California; Cornwall and Cumberland, England; Scotland; Russia; Brazil; Broken Hill, Australia.

*Aquamarine*

*Heliodor*

## CORDIERITE | $Mg_2Al_4Si_5O_{18}$ | Silicate

**Crystal System:** Orthorhombic

**Color:** Dark blue or gray-blue

**Transparency:** Transparent to translucent

**Luster:** Glassy

**Streak:** Colorless

**Hardness:** 7.0 to 7.5

**Habit:** Crystals rare; massive/granular; sometimes twinned

**Cleavage:** Poor in one direction

**Fracture:** Subconchoidal to uneven

**Specific Gravity:** 2.6 to 2.7 (increasing with increasing Iron content)

Cordierite is named for Pierre Louis Antoine Cordier, a nineteenth-century French geologist who first described the mineral; Cordier was also the first person to examine minerals using a microscope. **USE:** Transparent cordierite has been used as a gem called *saphir d'eau*. **ENVIRONMENT:** Widely distributed in sedimentary rock, in hydrothermal veins in association with sphalerite, pyrite, chalcopyrite, tetrahedrite, quartz, dolomite, barite, and fluorite; less frequently in pegmatites. **OCCURRENCE:** California; Idaho; Colorado; South Dakota; Connecticut; New Hampshire; Canada; Finland; Greenland; Scotland; England; Japan; Australia.

## CHRYSOCOLLA | $(Cu^{+2},Al)_2H_2Si_2O_5(OH)_4 \cdot nH_2O$     *Silicate*

**Crystal System:** Monoclinic

**Color:** Sky-blue to greenish blue or green, often streaked with black

**Transparency:** Translucent to almost opaque

**Luster:** Glassy, dull, or earthy

**Streak:** White to pale blue

**Hardness:** 2.0 to 4.0

**Habit:** Globular or compact

**Cleavage:** N/A

**Fracture:** Conchoidal

**Specific Gravity:** 2.0 to 2.4

The name comes from the Greek *chrysos*, for gold, and *kolla*, meaning glue; it looks similar to another material used as a flux in soldering gold. **USE:** A minor ore of copper, it has been used for cabochon jewelry but is very fragile and likely to crack as it loses water. **ENVIRONMENT:** Oxidized zones of copper deposits. **OCCURRENCE:** Pennsylvania; Michigan; Arizona; New Mexico; California; Utah; Mexico; England; Chile; Katanga, Zaire.

## ENSTATITE | $Mg_2Si_2O_6$     *Silicate (Pyroxine Group)*

**Crystal System:** Orthorhombic

**Color:** Pale green, yellow- or green-white, or brown

**Transparency:** Transparent to nearly opaque

**Luster:** Glassy

**Streak:** None to grayish

**Hardness:** 5.5 to 6.0

**Habit:** Massive/granular

**Cleavage:** Good in two directions lengthwise at nearly ninety degrees

**Fracture:** Uneven

**Specific Gravity:** 3.2 to 3.9

The name comes from the Greek *enstates*, meaning opponent, because this mineral has a refractory nature. Enstatite is a member of the pyroxene group, an important group of rock-forming minerals with the same general formula and two characteristic cleavages. **USE:** None. **ENVIRONMENT:** Enstatite and similar pyroxenes occur in igneous rocks, such as gabbros and pyroxenites, and in some andesitic volcanic rocks and stony meteorites. **OCCURRENCE:** Tilly Foster Mine, Brewster, New York; Pennsylvania; Colorado; Montana; Arizona; Maryland; Texas; Ireland; Scotland; Austria; Finland; Japan; South Africa.

## DIOPSIDE | $CaMgSi_2O_6$     *Silicate (Pyroxine Group)*

**Crystal System:** Monoclinic

**Color:** Grayish white, light green, or dark green

**Transparency:** Translucent to opaque

**Luster:** Glassy

**Streak:** White, grayish, or greenish

**Hardness:** 5.0 to 6.0

**Habit:** Massive/granular or prismatic; twinning common

**Cleavage:** Good in two directions lengthwise at nearly ninety degrees

**Fracture:** Uneven

**Specific Gravity:** 3.3 to 3.5

The name diopside comes from the Greek words *dis*, for double, and *opsis*, for view, because two views can be taken of its prismatic form. Diopside is a member of the pyroxene group. **USE:** Transparent diopsides have been cut for use as gemstones, but mainly for collectors rather than for jewelry. **ENVIRONMENT:** Found in metamorphosed impure limestones. **OCCURRENCE:** California; South Dakota; Colorado; Tennessee; Pennsylvania; New York; New Jersey; Quebec; Sweden; Switzerland; Italy; Finland; Russia; Korea; Japan.

## HEDENBERGITE | $CaFe^{+2}Si_2O_6$     *Silicate (Pyroxine Group)*

**Crystal System:** Monoclinic

**Color:** Brownish to grayish green, dark green, or black

**Transparency:** Translucent to opaque

**Luster:** Glassy

**Streak:** Greenish or brownish gray

**Hardness:** 5.0 to 6.0

**Habit:** Prismatic or massive/granular; twinning common

**Cleavage:** Perfect in two directions lengthwise at nearly ninety degrees

**Fracture:** Conchoidal

**Specific Gravity:** 3.3 to 3.5

Hedenbergite is named for M. A. Ludwig Hedenberg, the nineteenth-century Swedish chemist who analyzed and described the mineral. It is a member of the pyroxene group. **USE:** None. **ENVIRONMENT:** Found in igneous rocks and contact metamorphosed iron-rich sediments in association with ilvaite and magnetite. **OCCURRENCE:** California; Arizona; New Mexico; Utah; Idaho; New York; New Jersey; Greenland; England; Sweden; Italy; Australia.

## AUGITE | $(Ca,Na)(Mg,Fe,Al,Ti)(Si,Al)_2O_6$ — Silicate (Pyroxine Group)

**Crystal System:** Monoclinic

**Color:** Black

**Transparency:** Translucent (only thinnest pieces)

**Luster:** Glassy

**Streak:** Green or white

**Hardness:** 5.0 to 6.0

**Habit:** Massive/granular or prismatic; twinning common

**Cleavage:** Perfect in two directions lengthwise at nearly ninety degrees

**Fracture:** Uneven

**Specific Gravity:** 3.2 to 3.4

The name comes from the Greek *auge*, meaning bright, because of the luster of augite's cleavage planes. It is the most common member of the pyroxene group. **USE:** Most important ferromagnesian mineral found in igneous rocks, especially in basic and ultrabasic rocks. **ENVIRONMENT:** A common mineral in igneous rocks such as gabbros, basalts, and pyroxenites. **OCCURRENCE:** California; Oregon; Montana; Nevada; New York; New Hampshire; Canada; Greenland; Norway; Italy; India; Japan.

## RHODONITE | $(Mn^{+2},Fe^{+2},Mg,Ca)SiO_3$ — Silicate

**Crystal Systems:** Triclinic

**Color:** Pink to brown; weathers to black

**Transparency:** Transparent to translucent

**Luster:** Glassy

**Streak:** White

**Hardness:** 5.5 to 6.0

**Habit:** Crystals rare; tabular, prismatic, massive/granular, or compact

**Cleavage:** Good in two directions at nearly ninety degrees

**Fracture:** Uneven to conchoidal

**Specific Gravity:** 3.4 to 3.7

The name comes from the Greek word *rhodon*, meaning rose. **USE:** Rhodonite from Russia's Ural Mountains has been polished and used as a decorative stone. **ENVIRONMENT:** Usually found in hydrothermal veins in association with manganese ore deposits or in regionally metamorphosed manganese-containing sediments. **OCCURRENCE:** Fine fowlerite crystals found at Franklin, New Jersey. Also found in Massachusetts; California; Sweden; Russia; Finland; Italy; Germany; Romania; Brazil; India; South Africa; Broken Hill, Australia; Arrow Valley, New Zealand; Japan.

## TREMOLITE | $Ca_2(Mg,Fe^{+2})_5Si_8O_{22}(OH)_2$     Silicate (Amphibole Group)

| | |
|---|---|
| **Crystal System:** Monoclinic | |
| **Color:** White, light green, gray, or violet (hexagonite) | |
| **Transparency:** Transparent to translucent | |
| **Luster:** Glassy | |
| **Streak:** White | |
| **Hardness:** 5.0 to 6.0 | |
| **Habit:** Bladed, prismatic, fibrous, or massive; twinning common | |
| **Cleavage:** Perfect in two directions at approximately 120 degrees | |
| **Fracture:** Uneven | |
| **Specific Gravity:** 3.0 to 3.3 | |

Tremolite is named after the place where it was discovered— Val Tremola, near St. Gotthard, Switzerland. It is a member of the amphibole group, an important group of rock-forming minerals that have the same general formula and two characteristic cleavages. Some nephrite jade is also tremolite. Mountain cork (which is light enough to float on water) and mountain leather are two asbestos varieties of tremolite. **USE:** Fibrous varieties are used in fireproofing and in making electrical insulators. **ENVIRONMENT:** Found in thermally metamorphosed silica-rich dolomites or limestones. **OCCURRENCE:** Edwards, New York (hexagonite); Canaan, Connecticut; Lee, Massachusetts; California; Arizona; Utah; Colorado; Ontario; Quebec; Italy; Switzerland.

## HORNBLENDE | $Ca_2(Mg,Fe^{+2})_4Al(Si_7Al)O_{22}(OH,F)_2$     Silicate (Amphibole Group)

| | |
|---|---|
| **Crystal System:** Monoclinic | |
| **Color:** Dark green to black | |
| **Transparency:** Translucent to almost opaque | |
| **Luster:** Glassy | |
| **Streak:** Gray-green or gray-brown | |
| **Hardness:** 5.0 to 6.0 | |
| **Habit:** Prismatic, columnar, massive/granular, fibrous, or radiating | |
| **Cleavage:** Good in two directions at approximately 120 degrees | |
| **Fracture:** Uneven, splintery | |
| **Specific Gravity:** 3.0 to 3.4 | |

The name hornblende comes from two German words: a miner's term, *horn*, possibly referring to the color of horn; and *blende*, meaning a deceiver. Perhaps this is because the mineral is dark, shiny, and found with metallic ores but contains no valuable metal itself. The term hornblende describes two separate minerals, ferrohornblende and magnesio-hornblende, which are impossible to tell apart without chemical testing. Hornblende is a member of the amphibole group. **USE:** None. **ENVIRONMENT:** Common in many igneous rocks, including granodiorites and diorites. **OCCURRENCE:** California; Arizona; Idaho; Pennsylvania; Canada; Scotland; England; Korea; Japan; Australia; New Zealand.

## APOPHYLLITE | $KCa_4Si_8O_{20}(F,OH)$ — Silicate

**Crystal System:** Tetragonal or orthorhombic

**Color:** Colorless, white, pale pink, or pale green to emerald-green

**Transparency:** Transparent to translucent

**Luster:** Glassy; pearly parallel to cleavage

**Streak:** White

**Hardness:** 4.5 to 5.0

**Habit:** Prismatic or massive/granular

**Cleavage:** Perfect in one direction

**Fracture:** Uneven

**Specific Gravity:** 2.3 to 2.4

The name comes from the Greek *apo*, meaning away, and *phyllazein*, meaning to leaf, referring to apophyllite's tendency to exfoliate when heated with a blow-pipe flame. The term apophyllite describes three separate minerals, fluorapophyllite, hydroxyapophyllite, and natroapophyllite, which are almost impossible to tell apart without chemical testing. Fluorapophyllite is the most common of the three minerals. **USE:** None. **ENVIRONMENT:** Found as a secondary mineral in cavities in basalts and limestones in association with zeolites. **OCCURRENCE:** Brush Canyon, Los Angeles County, California; Table Mountain, Jefferson County, Colorado; Lake Superior, Michigan; Pennsylvania; Connecticut; New Jersey; Canada; Scotland; Sweden; Iceland; Germany; Mexico; India.

## TALC | $Mg_3Si_4O_{10}(OH)_2$ — Silicate

**Crystal System:** Monoclinic

**Color:** White to pale green or gray; may be stained red

**Transparency:** Translucent to opaque

**Luster:** Greasy to pearly

**Streak:** White

**Hardness:** 1.0

**Habit:** Massive/granular, foliated, or fibrous

**Cleavage:** Perfect in one direction

**Fracture:** N/A

**Specific Gravity:** 2.7 to 2.8

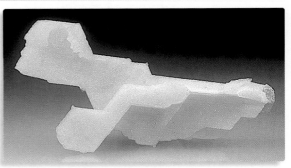

The name comes from the Arabic *talq*, for pure, probably referring to talc's white powder. **USE:** Massive talc is called steatite or soapstone. It was used by the Babylonians and Egyptians and is now used by the Inuit for carvings; ground talc produces talcum powder. **ENVIRONMENT:** A secondary mineral formed from the alteration of olivine, pyroxenes, and amphiboles; also found in metamorphosed magnesian rocks. **OCCURRENCE:** California; Arizona; Colorado; South Dakota; Vermont; Pennsylvania; New Hampshire; Thetford and Asbestos, Quebec; England; Norway; Sweden; France; Italy; South Africa; India; China; Australia.

## MUSCOVITE | $KAl_2(Si_3Al)O_{10}(OH,F)_2$

*Silicate (Mica Group)*

**Crystal System:** Monoclinic

**Color:** Colorless, white, pale gray, green, or brown

**Transparency:** Transparent to translucent

**Luster:** Glassy; pearly parallel to cleavage

**Streak:** Colorless

**Hardness:** 2.5 to 3.0

**Habit:** Tabular, foliated, flaky, scaly, or fibrous; twinning common

**Cleavage:** Perfect in one direction

**Fracture:** N/A

**Specific Gravity:** 2.8 to 2.9

The name muscovite is derived from its use in windows as Muscovy-glass, after the old Russian province. Muscovite is the pale (usually white or pale gray) member of the mica group. The term mica probably comes from the Latin *micare*, meaning to shine. **USE:** As an insulator in electrical equipment; as Christmas tree "snow"; as the thin transparent pieces set into stove doors or lantern windows. **ENVIRONMENT:** Widely distributed in all types of rocks, common in alkali granites and associated pegmatites; as a secondary mineral from the decomposition of feldspars, in schists and gneisses, and in clastic sandstones. **OCCURRENCE:** Large deposits at Black Hills, South Dakota; California; Colorado; New Mexico; New Hampshire; Maine; Connecticut; North Carolina; Ontario. Also found in Norway; Switzerland; Brazil; India.

## BIOTITE | $K(Mg,Fe^{+2})_3(Al,Fe^{+3})Si_3O_{10}(OH,F)_2$

*Silicate (Mica Group)*

**Crystal System:** Monoclinic

**Color:** Black, dark brown, or greenish black

**Transparency:** Transparent to translucent

**Luster:** Glassy to submetallic; pearly on cleavage surface

**Streak:** Colorless

**Hardness:** 2.5 to 3

**Habit:** Tabular (barrel-shaped), platy, or scaly

**Cleavage:** Perfect in one direction

**Fracture:** N/A

**Specific Gravity:** 2.8 to 3.4

Biotite is named for Jean Baptiste Biot, a nineteenth-century French physicist and chemist who first called attention to the optical differences among the different micas. Biotite is the dark black to brown member of the mica group. **USE:** None. **ENVIRONMENT:** Less common than muscovite, biotite is found in granites, pegmatites, schists, and gneisses. **OCCURRENCE:** California; New Mexico; Idaho; South Dakota; Alaska; Connecticut; Maine; Canada; Ireland; Sweden; Norway; Italy; Japan; New Zealand.

## LEPIDOLITE | $K(Li,Al)_3(Si,Al)_4O_{10}(F,OH)_2$ — *Silicate (Mica Group)*

**Crystal System:** Monoclinic

**Color:** Pale lilac, white, gray, or pale pink

**Transparency:** Transparent to translucent

**Luster:** Glassy; pearly on cleavage surfaces

**Streak:** Colorless

**Hardness:** 2.5 to 3.0

**Habit:** Tabular, often with pseudo-hexagonal outline; usually small disseminated flakes

**Cleavage:** Perfect in one direction

**Fracture:** N/A

**Specific Gravity:** 2.8 to 2.9

The name comes from the Greek word *lepidos*, meaning scale, because many lepidolite specimens appear scaly. Lepidolite is the pale lilac to pink member of the mica group. **USE:** A source for lithium. **ENVIRONMENT:** A relatively rare species, lepidolite is found in granite pegmatites in association with elbaite (lithium-tourmaline) and spodumene; less often in granites. **OCCURRENCE:** Pala District, San Diego County, California; Brown Derby Mine, Gunnison County, Colorado; South Dakota; Wyoming; New Mexico; Manitoba; Sweden; Germany; Finland; Mexico; Brazil.

## QUARTZ | $SiO_2$ — *Silicate*

**Crystal System:** Hexagonal

**Color:** Colorless, white (milky), black (smoky), pink (rose), purple (amethyst), yellow (citrine), or brown

**Transparency:** Transparent to translucent

**Luster:** Glassy

**Streak:** White

**Hardness:** 7.0

**Habit:** Prismatic, striated, or massive/granular; twinning common

**Cleavage:** N/A

**Fracture:** Conchoidal

**Specific Gravity:** 2.65

**Tests:** Soluble in hydrofluoric acid

*Milky Quartz*

*Amethyst*

*Smoky Quartz*

The origin of the name is uncertain: Possibly it came from the German *quarz*, itself of uncertain derivation; or from the West Slav *kwardy*, for hard; or from the Old English *querklufterz*, for cross-vein ore. Quartz became commonly known as crystal or rock crystal around the end of the eighteenth century. It is one of the most abundant of all the minerals. Crystalline quartz has many varieties; when pure, it is colorless (as in rock crystal), but it may be variously tinted: milky (white), smoky (black), rose (pink), amethyst (purple), or citrine (yellow). For cryptocrystalline quartz (such as chalcedony), see page 148. **USE:** As a semiprecious gemstone. **ENVIRONMENT:** One of the most widely distributed and important rock-forming minerals, quartz occurs in almost all types of rocks, including granites, gneisses, and clastic sediments; also in mineral veins and cavities where attractive crystals can be found; the rock quartzite is made almost entirely of

## QUARTZ | $SiO_2$ *(continued)*                                        *Silicate*

Rose Quartz

quartz. **OCCURRENCE:** Beautiful crystals are found at many localities, including: Hot Springs, Arkansas; Black Hills, South Dakota; Pike's Peak, Colorado; Auburn, Maine; Arizona; Montana; Iowa; Michigan; Virginia; New York; Pennsylvania; Canada; Scotland; England; Bourg d'Oissans, France; Italy; Switzerland; Mexico; Minas Gerais, Brazil; Japan; Australia.

## CHALCEDONY (QUARTZ) | $SiO_2$                                        *Silicate*

| | |
|---|---|
| **Crystal System:** Hexagonal | |
| **Color:** Variable, often banded; transparent | |
| **Transparency:** Transparent or translucent to opaque | |
| **Luster:** Glassy to waxy | |
| **Streak:** White | |
| **Hardness:** 6.5 to 7.0 | |
| **Habit:** Globular, massive, or nodular; sometimes banded | |
| **Cleavage:** N/A | |
| **Fracture:** Conchoidal | |
| **Specific Gravity:** 2.6 | |

Jasper

Chalcedony is the variety name given to fine cryptocrystalline quartz. In this variety, crystals are too small to be seen with the unaided eye or even with an ordinary microscope. Instead, the crystallinity can be determined with the use of an electron microscope. Chalcedony occurs in almost any color or combination of colors. Varieties include agate (colored bands), moss agate (milky-white background with dendritic green or brown inclusions), carnelian (red to reddish brown), sard (light to dark brown), chrysoprase (apple-green) bloodstone or heliotrope (green with red flecks), tiger's eye (banded yellow-brown), jasper (opaque red), and flint or chert (white, dull gray, or black). (For crystalline quartz, such as amethyst, see page 146). **USE:** As a

Agate

Chalcedony

semiprecious gemstone. **ENVIRONMENT:** Chalcedony solidifies from silica-rich solutions, usually in veins or cavities; chert and flint are formed by the deposition of silica from seawater or by the replacement of limestone by silica. **OCCURRENCE:** Florida; Oregon; Colorado; Nevada; Arizona; New Brunswick; England; Germany; Mexico; India; South Africa; Brazil.

---

**OPAL** | $SiO_2 \cdot nH_2O$           *Silicate*

| |
|---|
| **Crystal System:** Amorphous |
| **Color:** Variable, usually pale colors: white, milky, gray, red, brown, blue to black |
| **Transparency:** Transparent to translucent |
| **Luster:** Glassy to resinous; sometimes pearly |
| **Streak:** White |
| **Hardness:** 5.5 to 6.5 |
| **Habit:** Massive, may be stalactitic, globular, or compact |
| **Cleavage:** N/A |
| **Fracture:** Conchoidal |
| **Specific Gravity:** 1.9 to 2.2 |

The name comes from the Greek *opalios* or Sanskrit *upala*, for gem or precious stone. It is closely related to quartz, but is amorphous (no crystal structure) and contains up to 10 percent water. It is one of only two gemstones (amber being the other) that are amorphous. **USE:** Milky-white or black opals with a play of spectral color are used as gemstones; in some cases, very fine black precious opals can rival diamonds in price. The variety diatomaceous earth is used as an abrasive, filler, filtration powder, or insulator. **ENVIRONMENT:** Deposited at low temperatures from silica-rich waters in fissures and cavities in all kinds of rocks; common around geysers and hot springs; also formed during weathering of rocks; also makes up skeletons of sponges and diatoms. **OCCURRENCE:** Virgin Valley, Nevada (precious opal); California (diatomaceous earth); Washington; Oregon; Idaho; Wyoming; Nebraska; Colorado; Arizona; Georgia; Mexico (gem opal). The world's most valuable opals come from Queensland and New South Wales, Australia.

## ORTHOCLASE | KAISi₃O₈

*Silicate (Feldspar Group)*

| | |
|---|---|
| **Crystal System:** Monoclinic | |
| **Color :** White, flesh-pink, or (rarely) red | |
| **Transparency:** Translucent | |
| **Luster:** Glassy; pearly parallel to cleavage | |
| **Streak:** White | |
| **Hardness:** 6.0 to 6.5 | |
| **Habit:** Massive/granular or tabular; twinning common | |
| **Cleavage:** Good in two directions at nearly ninety degrees | |
| **Fracture:** Conchoidal | |
| **Specific Gravity:** 2.5 to 2.6 | |

The name comes from the Greek word *orthos*, meaning right, and *klas*, meaning to break, alluding to its two prominent cleavages at nearly right angles. **USE:** Used in the manufacture of porcelain; when fused, it provides part of the glaze used on porcelain. Small amounts may be used in the production of glass. **ENVIRONMENT:** Found as a major constituent of plutonic rocks such as pegmatites, granites, and syenites; in schists and other metamorphic rocks; in hydrothermal ore veins and in some arkose sandstones. **OCCURRENCE:** Crystal Peak and Pike's Peak, Colorado; Amelia, Virginia; Alaska; California; Nevada; Idaho; Texas; New York; Pennsylvania; Canada; England; France; Norway; Switzerland; Madagascar; Mexico; Korea; Japan.

## MICROCLINE | KAISi₃O₈

*Silicate (Feldspar Group)*

| | |
|---|---|
| **Crystal System:** Triclinic | |
| **Color:** White, gray, flesh-colored, red-brown, or green (amazonite) | |
| **Transparency:** Translucent | |
| **Luster:** Glassy; pearly parallel to cleavage | |
| **Streak:** White | |
| **Hardness:** 6.0 to 6.5 | |
| **Habit:** Prismatic or massive/granular; twinning common | |
| **Cleavage:** Good in two directions at nearly ninety degrees | |
| **Fracture:** Uneven | |
| **Specific Gravity:** 2.5 to 2.6 | |

The name comes from the Greek *micro*, for small, and *keinen*, meaning to incline, referring to the small deviation from ninety degrees of its intersecting cleavage planes. **USE:** Used in the manufacture of porcelain; when fused, it provides part of the glaze used on porcelain. Small amounts may be used in the production of glass. **ENVIRONMENT:** Found as a major constituent of plutonic rocks, such as pegmatites, granites, and syenites. **OCCURRENCE:** Rutherford Mines, near Amelia, Virginia; Brown Derby Mine, Gunnison County, and Pike's Peak area, Colorado; Tin Mountain and Ingersoll mines, Black Hills, South Dakota; New Mexico; California; Canada; Norway; Greenland; Finland; France; Madagascar; Japan; Australia.

## ALBITE | $NaAlSi_3O_8$                   Silicate (Feldspar Group)

| | |
|---|---|
| **Crystal System:** Triclinic | |
| **Color:** White, yellow, or reddish gray to black | |
| **Transparency:** Transparent to translucent | |
| **Luster:** Glassy | |
| **Streak:** White | |
| **Hardness:** 6.0 | |
| **Habit:** Tabular, platy, scaly, or massive/granular; twinning very common | |
| **Cleavage:** Good in two directions at nearly ninety degrees; poor in two directions | |
| **Fracture:** Conchoidal | |
| **Specific Gravity:** 2.6 to 2.8 | |

The name comes from the Latin *albus*, meaning white; albite usually is white. Albite is a member of the plagioclase series, a complete series from albite to anorthite, with members in between made up of differing amounts of sodium and calcium. **USE:** Manufacture of ceramics. **ENVIRONMENT:** Found in plutonic rocks such as pegmatites. **OCCURRENCE:** Virginia; Maine; Connecticut; Canada; England; Norway; France; Germany; Mexico; India; Pakistan; Brazil; Japan.

## LABRADORITE | (Ca,Na) $AlSi_3O_8$                   Silicate (Feldspar Group)

| | |
|---|---|
| **Crystal System:** Triclinic | |
| **Color, Transparency:** Blue, green, white, gray, or black | |
| **Transparency:** Transparent to translucent | |
| **Luster:** Glassy | |
| **Streak:** White | |
| **Hardness:** 6.0 | |
| **Habit:** Tabular, massive/granular, or compact; twinning common | |
| **Cleavage:** Good in two directions at nearly ninety degrees | |
| **Fracture:** Conchoidal | |
| **Specific Gravity:** 2.6 to 2.8 | |

Labradorite is named for the place where it was discovered: Isle of Paul, Nain, in Labrador, Canada. It is an intermediary member of the plagioclase series, containing more calcium than sodium. **USE:** Polished and used as building face stones and in cabochon jewelry. **ENVIRONMENT:** Found in igneous and metamorphic rocks such as anorthosites, andesites, basalts, and diorites. **OCCURRENCE:** California; Utah; Oregon; New York. Beautiful specimens found in Labrador. Also found in Norway; Sweden; Greenland; Russia; Mexico.

## SODALITE | $Na_8Al_6Si_6O_{24}Cl_2$ — Silicate

**Crystal System:** Isometric

**Color:** Usually azure-blue; may be white, yellow, green, or pink (hackmanite)

**Transparency:** Transparent to translucent

**Luster:** Glassy

**Streak:** White

**Hardness:** 5.5 to 6.0

**Habit:** Crystals rare; massive/granular

**Cleavage:** Poor in six directions

**Fracture:** Conchoidal to uneven

**Specific Gravity:** 2.2 to 2.3

The name sodalite refers to its sodium content. **USE:** As a cabochon gemstone. **ENVIRONMENT:** In igneous rocks such as nepheline syenite and in dikes and sills that are low in silica; in association with nepheline and cancrinite. **OCCURRENCE:** Bearpaw Mountains, Montana; Lawrence County, South Dakota; Cripple Creek, Colorado; Magnet Cove, Arkansas (hackmanite); Bancroft, Ontario; Mont St. Hilaire, Quebec; Kicking Horse Pass, British Columbia; Vesuvius in Sicily, Italy (transparent crystals); Greenland; Scotland; Norway; Germany; Russia; Bolivia; Zambia.

## LAZURITE | $(Na, Ca)_{7-8}(Al,Si)_{12}(O,S)_{24}[(SO_4),Cl_2,(OH)_2]$ — Silicate

**Crystal System:** Isometric

**Color:** Azure-blue to violet-blue

**Transparency:** Translucent

**Luster:** Glassy

**Streak:** Bright blue

**Hardness:** 5.0 to 5.5

**Habit:** Crystals rare; massive/granular

**Cleavage:** Poor in six directions

**Fracture:** Uneven

**Specific Gravity:** 2.4 to 2.5

The name is derived from a variety of words meaning blue or heaven: the Latin *lazulum*, the Arabic *lazaward*, and the Persian *lazhuward*. **USE:** Once powdered to make the pigment ultramarine (a synthetic lazurite is now used). Lapis lazuli, (a mixture of lazurite, calcite, pyrite, and diopside) is polished to make gemstones. **ENVIRONMENT:** Forms in association with pyrite, calcite, and diopside in contact metamorphic rocks. **OCCURRENCE:** Cascade Canyon, San Bernardino County, California; North Italian Mountain, Gunnison County, Colorado; Lake Baikal, Siberia; the Andes near Ovalle, Chile. Some of the world's most beautiful lazurite (lapis lazuli) is found in the Kokcha River valley, Badakhstan, Afghanistan.

## SCAPOLITE | $(Na,Ca)_4Al_3(Al,Si)_3Si_6O_{24}(Cl,CO_3,SO_4)$     *Silicate*

| | |
|---|---|
| **Crystal System:** Tetragonal | |
| **Color:** Colorless, white to bluish gray, pink, yellow, or brown | |
| **Transparency:** Transparent to translucent | |
| **Luster:** Glassy to pearly | |
| **Streak:** White | |
| **Hardness:** 5.5 to 6.0 | |
| **Habit:** Prismatic or massive/granular | |
| **Cleavage:** Distinct in two directions | |
| **Fracture:** Conchoidal to uneven | |
| **Specific Gravity:** 2.5 to 2.7 | |

The name comes from the Greek *skapos*, meaning shaft, referring to the prismatic shape of the crystals. Scapolite is a group with two members: marialite and meionite. They both have similar properties and are difficult to tell apart without chemical testing. **USE:** None. **ENVIRONMENT:** In metamorphic rocks, most commonly in metamorphosed limestones, and replacing feldspars in altered igneous rocks. **OCCURRENCE:** Rossie and Pierrepont, St. Lawrence County, New York; Bedford and Renfrew, Ontario; Quebec; Italy; Norway; Finland; Russia; Madagascar; Burma.

## STILBITE | $NaCa_2Al_5Si_{13}O_{36} \cdot 14H_2O$     *Silicate*

| | |
|---|---|
| **Crystal System:** Monoclinic | |
| **Color:** White, yellow, pink, or (sometimes) brick-red | |
| **Transparency:** Transparent to translucent | |
| **Luster:** Glassy; pearly on cleavage surfaces | |
| **Streak:** Colorless | |
| **Hardness:** 3.5 to 4.0 | |
| **Habit:** Prismatic, striated, compact, fibrous, or massive/granular | |
| **Cleavage:** Perfect in one direction | |
| **Fracture:** Uneven | |
| **Specific Gravity:** 2.1 to 2.2 | |

The name comes from the Greek word *stilbein*, meaning to glitter or shine, or *stilbe*, a mirror, referring to the mineral's pearly or glassy luster. Stilbite is a zeolite, a group of minerals that can lose and gain water very easily. **USE:** None. **ENVIRONMENT:** In cavities in basalts and related rocks, often in association with the mineral heulandite. **OCCURRENCE:** Cowlitz County, Washington; Oregon; California; Montgomery County, Pennsylvania; Paterson and Great Notch, New Jersey; Connecticut; Nova Scotia; Scotland; Norway; Italy; Germany; India; Mexico; Brazil; Japan.

# Rock Identification Guide

The rocks in this section have been grouped according to the three major rock types: igneous, sedimentary, and metamorphic.

## GRANITE                                                    *Igneous*

**Group:** Igneous

**Classification:** Acidic

**Origin:** Intrusive

**Mineral Composition:** Quartz, potassium feldspars, and plagioclase feldspars dominant; minor amounts of biotite, muscovite, and hornblende

Granite is an intrusive igneous rock found at Earth's surface. Granitic rock forms the core of many mountain ranges—such as the Rockies, the Himalayas, and the Alps—and is the most common rock in the Precambrian shields of Canada, Siberia, Scandinavia, and Brazil. Granite's resistance to erosion has created some of the world's most famous landmarks—for example, Mount Rushmore, South Dakota, and Sugar Loaf Mountain, Brazil. Apatite, hematite, magnetite, garnet, and pyrite are commonly associated with granitic intrusions. **USE:** Because of its hardness and resistance to weathering, granite is often the material of choice for buildings and monuments. **APPEARANCE:** Light-colored rock (white to light gray, sometimes pink) with medium- to coarse-grained texture. **ORIGIN:** Slow cooling and crystallization of silica-rich magmas form huge batholiths at considerable depth in Earth's crust.

## FELDSPAR PEGMATITE                                        *Igneous*

**Group:** Igneous

**Classification:** Acidic

**Origin:** Intrusive

**Mineral Composition:** Acidic rocks with same mineral composition as granite

The largest mineral crystals ever recorded (some weighing more than five tons) come from pegmatite rocks. They are found worldwide in dikes, veins, and other small igneous intrusions. Gem-quality microcline feldspar pegmatite specimens are found in the Ural Mountains and Pike's Peak, Colorado, while beautiful plagioclase feldspar pegmatite deposits occur in Madagascar and in eastern Canada. Large, well-formed crystals are associated with pegmatites, including andalusite, beryl, chrysoberyl, topaz, and tourmaline. **USE:** Large feldspar pegmatite deposits are mined for use in manufacturing ceramics, glass, space-age resins, and epoxies. **APPEARANCE:** Very coarse grained with some specimens containing crystals many feet long; color varies according to type of feldspar present. **ORIGIN:** Minerals crystallize from fluids and gases concentrated from underlying cooling magma intrusions.

## NEPHELINE SYENITE

*Igneous*

**Group:** Igneous

**Classification:** Intermediate

**Origin:** Intrusive

**Mineral Composition:**
Potassium feldspars, sodium-rich plagioclase feldspars, and nepheline characteristic minerals; quartz absent

The name syenite is derived from the Egyptian city of Aswan, which was formerly known as Syene. It is a fairly rare rock that resembles granite in appearance and texture, but contains no quartz. Extensive nepheline syenite deposits are currently being mined in Arkansas, New Mexico, Quebec, Ontario, Norway, Brazil, and Australia. Minerals found with nepheline syenites include albite, apatite, magnetite, and titanite. **USE:** Ceramics, rock-wool insulation, building facings, floor tiles, and memorials. **APPEARANCE:** Medium- to coarse-grained rock; light to medium gray in color with a blue tint. **ORIGIN:** Forms in dikes, sills, and other minor igneous intrusions; in border zones of larger granitic bodies.

## GRANODIORITE

*Igneous*

**Group:** Igneous

**Classification:** Intermediate

**Origin:** Intrusive

**Mineral Composition:**
Abundant quartz and plagioclase; lesser quantities of potassium feldspar, hornblende, and biotite

Granodiorite is a widespread acidic intrusive rock of similar mineral composition to granite, except for a higher proportion of plagioclase feldspar to potassium feldspar. Beautiful samples of granodiorite can be found in California, Japan, Norway, Austria, and Romania. Granodiorite acts as a host rock for many ore-bearing veins, including gold, cassiterite, wolframite, chalcopyrite, and sphalerite. **USE:** Building materials, polished slabs, ornamental stone, and road stone aggregate. **APPEARANCE:** Coarse-grained rock that is light gray in color with small dark speckles of biotite and hornblende. **ORIGIN:** Forms in every type of igneous intrusion, especially batholiths.

## DIORITE
*Igneous*

**Group:** Igneous

**Classification:** Intermediate

**Origin:** Intrusive

**Mineral Composition:** Composed predominantly of plagioclase feldspars and ferromagnesian minerals (hornblende, augite, biotite); quartz and potassium feldspars usually absent

Diorite is an intermediate igneous rock composed of equal amounts of light felsic minerals and dark ferromagnesian minerals. Excellent examples can be found in California, Canada, France, Germany, and Scandinavia. Almandine, apatite, magnetite, and titanite are some of the minerals associated with diorite intrusions. **USE:** Building face stone; polished slabs. **APPEARANCE:** Medium- to coarse-grained texture, with a salt-and-pepper appearance from the presence of white to light gray plagioclase and dark ferromagnesian minerals. **ORIGIN:** Forms from slow-cooling magmas richer in iron and magnesium than those that produce granites; commonly intruded as sills and dikes, and in the border zones of granite batholiths.

## GABBRO
*Igneous*

**Group:** Igneous

**Classification:** Basic

**Origin:** Intrusive

**Mineral Composition:** Ferromagnesians dominant, with pyroxenes (augite) in equal or greater proportions than plagioclase; hornblende and olivine present

Silica-poor, but rich in ferromagnesian minerals, gabbro is an intrusive rock that is not very common in Earth's continental crust, but is the main constituent of oceanic crust. Outcrops can be seen in New York, Ontario, Greenland, South Africa, and Scandinavia. Some gabbros are associated with large ore bodies, such as those in Sudbury, Ontario, and Kiruna, Sweden. **USE:** Crushed stone for concrete aggregate and railroad ballast; cut and polished for face stone. **APPEARANCE:** Medium- to coarse-grained texture; greenish gray to dark depending on amount of ferromagnesian minerals. **ORIGIN:** Forms by slow cooling and crystallization of a magma that has less silica than a granite magma; occurs as large dikes and batholiths.

## PERIODOTITE

*Igneous*

**Group:** Igneous

**Classification:** Ultrabasic

**Origin:** Intrusive

**Mineral Composition:** Olivine and pyroxenes primary minerals

Peridotite, formed in Earth's upper mantle, is a dark, dense igneous rock containing abundant iron and magnesium. It occurs worldwide, but particularly in New Zealand, South Africa, Ontario, and the eastern U.S.—for example, New York, Kentucky, and Georgia. Peridotites are a valuable source of ores and minerals, including chromite, platinum, nickel, and garnet. Mica-rich peridotites in South Africa, Canada, and Brazil are a good source of diamonds. **USE:** None. **APPEARANCE:** Coarse-grained texture; olive green to black in color. **ORIGIN:** Slow cooling and crystallization of a magma of ferromagnesian-silica composition, often brought to the surface from great depths by volcanic activity; occurs as small intrusions, sills, and dikes.

## RHYOLITE

*Igneous*

**Group:** Igneous

**Classification:** Acidic

**Origin:** Extrusive

**Mineral Composition:** Mineralogy too small to see with naked eye, but includes quartz, potassium feldspar, biotite, and hornblende

Rhyolite is the extrusive equivalent of granite and, like granite, it is found worldwide, most commonly in areas with acidic magma-tism—California, Arizona, Utah, Mexico, Japan, and Ethiopia. Prominent mineral occurrences associated with rhyolites include biotite, opal, magnetite, and topaz. **USE:** As a road stone aggregate. **APPEARANCE:** Buff to grayish color with a very fine-grained texture; commonly has quartz phenocrysts, with the phenocrysts aligned in the direction of flow. **ORIGIN:** Magmas of granitic composition that have erupted at Earth's surface or intruded at a shallow depth; forms small lava flows or intrusive bodies such as domes, dikes, and sills.

## PUMICE

**Group:** Igneous

**Classification:** Acidic

**Origin:** Extrusive

**Mineral Composition:** Glass froth of rhyolitic composition, with various silicate minerals and calcite as accessories

Pumice is a glassy volcanic rock that is so full of cavities it will float on water: After the eruption of the volcano Krakatoa in 1883, floating pumice rocks were a hazard to navigation on the Indian Ocean. Pumice is abundant on some islands of volcanic origin, including Lipari, Italy; Thiva, Greece; Indonesia; and Japan. **USE:** As abrasives and cleaning powders. **APPEARANCE:** White or creamy-white spongelike rock. **ORIGIN:** Develops when gas escapes through lava and forms a froth; some pumice forms as crusts on lava flows, some as particles erupted from volcanoes.

## TRACHYTE

**Group:** Igneous

**Classification:** Acidic

**Origin:** Extrusive

**Mineral Composition:** Plagioclase feldspars, sanidine feldspar, and hornblende essential minerals; quartz accounts for less than 5 percent

Trachyte is the volcanic equivalent of syenite rock; it forms from magma of syenitic composition. A relatively rare rock, its name is derived from the Greek *trakyte*, meaning rough, and refers to its ragged surface. Good examples can be seen in Hungary, New Zealand, and various volcanic islands in the Atlantic and Pacific oceans. Although very few interesting minerals are associated with trachyte deposits, one notable exception is topaz. **USE:** Building industry—for example, flooring, pavements, and external facings. **APPEARANCE:** A light-colored, fine-grained rock that exhibits a flow texture; occasional recognizable crystals of feldspar and hornblende may be scattered throughout the matrix. **ORIGIN:** Forms as small surface lava flows, small dikes, and other magma bodies intruded at shallow depths.

## ANDESITE

*Igneous*

**Group:** Igneous

**Classification:** Intermediate

**Origin:** Extrusive

**Mineral Composition:** Fine ground mass of plagioclase feldspars, with smaller amounts of hornblende, biotite, and augite; all of minerals may occur as phenocrysts

This rock was first described in the Andes mountains— hence its name. The volcanic equivalent of diorite, it is formed from magma of dioritic composition. It is abundant in oceanic-continental collision zones, such as the Andes, the Cascades, Indonesia, Japan, and other western Pacific volcanic islands. The world's largest copper ore deposits are associated with the andesites of western North and South America. **USE:** Road stone aggregate and building material. **APPEARANCE:** Fine bigranular texture that is often banded; crystals may be difficult to see except with a hand lens; color varies from green to brown-black, but is mostly medium gray. **ORIGIN:** Lava flows and small intrusions associated with volcanic mountain ranges.

## BASALT

*Igneous*

Basalt

Scoria

**Group:** Igneous

**Classification:** Basic

**Origin:** Extrusive

**Mineral Composition:** Pyroxene and plagioclase feldspar essential minerals; olivine often present

Basalt, the fine-grained equivalent of gabbro, is more abundant than all the other volcanic rocks combined. Basalt flows on continents can cover hundreds of thousands of square miles. Classic examples are located in the Columbia Basalt Plateau, western U.S., and the Deccan Traps, India. Many volcanic islands are also made up of basalt, including the great mass of rock forming the Hawaiian Islands. Agates, amethyst, silver, stibnite, native copper, and a host of other minerals are associated with basalts. **USE:** Road stone aggregate. **APPEARANCE:** Dark greenish gray to black with crystals that are generally too small to identify; vesicular structures commonly develop near the surface of lava flows, creating a variety of basalt called scoria. **ORIGIN:** Lava flows, sills, and dikes; associated with volcanic submarine flows.

## OBSIDIAN *Igneous*

*Black Obsidian*

*Snowflake Obsidian*

**Group:** Igneous

**Classification:** Acidic

**Origin:** Extrusive

**Mineral Composition:**
Glass essential component, with iron minerals as accessories; snowflake obsidian contains tabular crystals of potassium feldspar

Obsidian, or volcanic glass, is a rock that does not have a crystalline structure. Black obsidian is found in many parts of the world, the most famous occurrence being Obsidian Cliffs in Wyoming. A rare variety of obsidian prized among collectors is called snowflake obsidian. Some of the best collecting areas are in Utah. **USE:** In prehistoric times for making various tools and jewelry; snowflake obsidian is still used for jewelry. **APPEARANCE:** May be black, dark gray, red, or brown, with the color depending on the type of iron minerals present; breaks with the same conchoidal fracture as glass. **ORIGIN:** Hardened quickly s flows or fragments ejected by explosive volcanoes; if it had cooled slowly, it would have the same composition as rhyolite.

## TUFF *Igneous*

**Group:** Igneous

**Classification:** Acidic

**Origin:** Extrusive

**Mineral Composition:**
Volcanic ash and dust made of plagioclase, sanidine, quartz, micas, glassy shards, and rock fragments

Tuffs are pyroclastic rocks that form when volcanic ash becomes consolidated. Although tuffs are deposited in the same manner as sedimentary rocks, they are usually classified as volcanic because they consist of volcanic particles.

Deposits of tuff are found around volcanoes with histories of violent eruptions. An ancient volcano in the Crater Lakes region of Oregon was responsible for deposits of tuff that cover hundreds of thousands of square miles. **USE:** Cemented varieties used in building materials. **APPEARANCE:** Light-colored, fine-grained, very porous rock; vesicles sometimes filled with minerals that make the rock harder; commonly occurs in well-defined layers. **ORIGIN:** Accumulation of fine pyroclastic material ejected violently by explosive volcanic eruptions.

## CONGLOMERATE

*Sedimentary*

**Group:** Sedimentary

**Classification:** Detrital

**Grain Size:** Very coarse

**Mineral Composition:**
Fragments of different rocks and minerals, often quartzite, chert, and quartz; matrix consists of sand, cemented with silica, iron-oxide, or calcite

Conglomerates are very coarse-grained sedimentary rocks found in modern and ancient river valleys, alluvial fans, and beaches. They have been mined as a source of gold (in California, Alaska, and South Africa); for uranium (in South Africa and Canada); for copper (in Michigan); and for diamonds (in Australia). Other minerals associated with conglomerates include chromite, corundum, sapphire, and platinum. **USE:** Building materials, including cement. **APPEARANCE:** Gravel-sized, generally rounded pebbles that are embedded in fine- to medium-grained matrix; color depends on components. **ORIGIN:** Large rock fragments that are transported, rounded, and eventually deposited by swift-flowing streams, storm waves, or glacial ice.

## SEDIMENTARY BRECCIA

*Sedimentary*

**Group:** Sedimentary

**Classification:** Detrital

**Grain Size:** Very coarse

**Mineral Composition:**
Fragments can be any type of rock or mineral; matrix composed of sand, cemented with silica, iron-oxide, or calcite

Breccias are similar to conglomerates, except the rock fragments are angular instead of rounded. Breccias are found in association with scree slopes, cave-ins in karst areas, landslides, and fault fracture zones. Beautifully colored breccias are quarried in Morocco, Croatia, Slovenia, and Switzerland. In general, breccias are not a productive mineral environment. **USE:** Cement and ornamental stone. **APPEARANCE:** Large angular pieces of rock embedded in a sand and silt matrix; color varies according to the color of rock fragments. **ORIGIN:** Formed by the cementation of coarse angular rock fragments. The angular shape indicates fragments have not been transported very far from where they originally formed—the original sediment source area, as geologists term it.

## SANDSTONE

*Sedimentary*

**Group:** Sedimentary

**Classification:** Detrital

**Grain Size:** Medium

**Mineral Composition:** May be composed of any sand-sized mineral or rock fragment, but quartz dominant component; iron-oxide, silica, and calcite major cements

Sandstones are among the most common sedimentary rocks. They are the world's principal reservoir rocks for oil and gas deposits, also the principal aquifers for water. Spectacular viewing areas include the Grand Canyon, Colorado, and the carved sandstone city of Petra, Jordan. In general, they are not a productive mineral environment. **USE:** As building stones and in glass-making. **APPEARANCE:** Clastic texture (formed from broken pieces of older rocks), with mostly rounded, sand-sized grains; color depends on cementing agent and grains; fossils, bedding, and ripple marks are common. **ORIGIN:** Sand-sized sediments that have accumulated in a variety of environments including beaches, deltas, and deserts.

## GRAYWACKE

*Sedimentary*

**Group:** Sedimentary

**Classification:** Detrital

**Grain Size:** Medium or fine

**Mineral Composition:** Quartz, feldspars, and sand-sized rock fragments in almost equal amounts; considerable amounts of clay in matrix

Graywackes are essentially clay-rich sandstones that usually form in deep ocean environments. Good examples of graywacke rocks are found in England, Wales, Germany, Japan, and West Virginia. Usually they are not a productive mineral environment. **USE:** Building materials. **APPEARANCE:** Usually poorly sorted with a variety of grain sizes present; typically dark gray or green in color. **ORIGIN:** Deposited by turbidity currents, currents of dense sediment-laden water that move from the edge of the continental shelf into deeper water.

## SHALE

*Sedimentary*

**Group:** Sedimentary

**Classification:** Detrital

**Grain Size:** Fine

**Mineral Composition:**
Mixture of clay minerals, with detrital quartz, feldspar, and mica; minerals not visible to naked eye

Shale is character-ized by its ability to split into thin layers and flakes. Famous localities include the oil-bearing shales of Wyoming, the fossil-bearing Burgess Shales of western Canada, and the rich copper-and zinc-bearing Kupferschiefer Shales of northern Europe. Pyrite, gypsum, chal-copyrite, and celestite are associated minerals. **USE:** Brick and tile; also oil shales have enormous potential as a supply of fossil fuels. **APPEARANCE:** Very fine-grained with thin laminations; mud cracks and ripple marks are common; many shades of green, red, brown, gray, and black. **ORIGIN:** Accumulation of clay sediments deposited on lake or ocean bottom.

## MUDSTONE

*Sedimentary*

**Group:** Sedimentary

**Classification:** Detrital

**Grain Size:** Fine

**Mineral Composition:**
Minerals microscopic; include quartz, feldspars, and clays

Mudstones are similar to shales in grain size and mineral composition, but unlike shales they cannot be easily split along natural lines of cleavage. Mudstones occur in every part of the world, but their localities are seldom useful for collecting miner-als. **USE:** Manufacture of bricks, pottery, and other ceramics. **APPEARANCE:** Irregular orientation of clay particles leads to a massive and blocky appearance, with layers up to several feet thick; mudstones may break apart when wet; colors are variable and depend on clay component. **ORIGIN:** Silt and clay sediments deposited on lake or ocean bottom.

## ROCK SALT · *Sedimentary*

**Group:** Sedimentary

**Classification:** Chemical

**Grain Size:** Fine to medium

**Mineral Composition:** Mostly halite, with inclusions of gypsum, dolomite, and clay minerals

Rock salt is an evaporitic rock that forms in very arid environments and can attain immense thicknesses. Today rock salt is mined or quarried in more than seventy countries. Deposits in New Mexico and Germany, for example, are more than a thousand feet (305 m) thick. Dolomite, gypsum, and anhydrite are commonly associated minerals. **USE:** Essential material in human diet and chemical industry; massive underground domes are associated with fossil fuel and sulfur deposits. **APPEARANCE:** Massive, coarsely crystalline, with halite grains often large enough to be seen with the naked eye; white to colorless when pure, but impurities can produce gray, pink, blue, or yellow specimens. **ORIGIN:** Chemical evaporite deposits formed by the evaporation of salt-rich lakes or isolated bodies of seawater.

## LIMESTONE (FOSSILIFEROUS) · *Sedimentary*

**Group:** Sedimentary

**Classification:** Biochemical

**Grain Size:** Medium to fine

**Mineral Composition:** Dominant mineral calcite, with minor amounts of dolomite, clay, rock particles, and quartz

Limestone is a relatively soft rock made of calcium carbonate. It occurs all over the world and in a variety of forms, including chalk *(page 167)* and fossiliferous limestone *(left).* Made of fossilized organisms in reefs, fossiliferous limestone can be seen in all the great mountain chains of the world. Minerals associated with these limestones include calcite, pyrite, marcasite, manganite, and hematite. Fossilized limestones located in Saudi Arabia and Iran contain the world's largest oil and gas deposits. **USE:** Construction materials, including crushed stone and polished slabs. **APPEARANCE:** Abundant fossils, complete or fragmented, in a dense crystalline matrix of calcite or calcareous mud; usually white, light to dark gray, or black in color. **ORIGIN:** Formed from whole or broken fragments of various calcareous fossils deposited on the seafloor.

## DOLOMITE

*Sedimentary*

**Group:** Sedimentary

**Classification:** Chemical

**Grain Size:** Medium to fine

**Mineral Composition:** Composed almost entirely of mineral dolomite, with small amounts of calcite

Dolomite is the dominant rock in ancient reef deposits and is found worldwide. The classic locality is the massive reef and coral complex of the Dolomite Alps in Italy. Calcite, anhydrite, gypsum, sulfur, and barite may be found in pores of dolomite. **USE:** Preparation of cement and gravel; extraction of magnesium; flux in iron smelting. **APPEARANCE:** Compact homogeneous rock with visible mineral grains; various shades of white, pink, gray, and tan. **ORIGIN:** Magnesium-rich waters infiltrating limestones replaces calcium carbonate (calcite) with magnesium carbonate (dolomite).

## TRAVERTINE

*Sedimentary*

**Group:** Sedimentary

**Classification:** Chemical

**Grain Size:** Fine

**Mineral Composition:** Calcite or aragonite dominant mineral; minor amounts of limonite

Travertine has been the principal building stone in Rome since the Roman Empire and is now widely used throughout the world for decorative purposes. A limestone, it is found in caves and around hot or cold springs. Famous multicolored terraces are found in Yellowstone National Park; other localities include Turkey and the Czech Republic. No distinctive minerals are associated with travertine deposits. **USE:** Building materials for walls and floors. **APPEARANCE:** Compact porous rock with thin wavy laminae of oriented calcite crystals; white, yellowish, or rosy depending on limonite concentration. **ORIGIN:** Precipitation of calcite (calcium carbonate) from water.

## CHERT

**Group:** Sedimentary

**Classification:** Chemical

**Grain Size:** Microscopic

**Mineral Composition:**
Chalcedony and opal major components

Chert, a microcrystalline quartz, occurs as massive layered beds of silica rock that formed on the floor of ancient oceans. In places such as Oregon and California, the rock reaches thicknesses of more than eight hundred feet (244 m). Extensive deposits are also found in Germany, the Czech Republic, and Scotland. Associated minerals include pyrolusite and rhodochrosite. **USE:** None. **APPEARANCE:** Chert is very hard, with a microcrystalline texture and a conchoidal fracture; color is variable, ranging from green to red to brown. **ORIGIN:** Uncertain; possibly from precipitation of silica from seawater or accumulation of siliceous organisms on the ocean floor.

## FLINT

**Group:** Sedimentary

**Classification:** Chemical

**Grain Size:** Fine to microscopic

**Mineral Composition:**
Chalcedony and opal, with traces of marine microfossils

Flint is a special variety of chert that played an important role in the early history of humans, when it was used for making arrowheads, scrapers, knives, and other tools. Flint occurs as nodules or irregular lenses in chalk deposits and can be seen in the massive chalk outcrops of England, Germany, and Denmark. It is not associated with any particular mineral. **USE:** None. **APPEARANCE:** Very hard, with a microcrystalline texture and a conchoidal fracture; color varies from light gray to black, depending on content of organic matter. **ORIGIN:** From precipitation of silica in nodular shapes and thin layers in silica-rich limestones.

## COAL (BITUMINOUS)                    *Sedimentary*

**Group:** Sedimentary

**Classification:** Organic

**Grain Size:** Medium to fine

**Mineral Composition:**
Carbon, hydrogen, and
oxygen, with some sulfur

Bituminous coal is the most common variety of coal in the world. It is a solid rocklike fossil fuel, which is dusty to handle, ignites easily, and burns with a smoky flame. Most of the world's bituminous coal deposits are located in the northern hemisphere, with the U.S., Russia, and China holding the largest reserves. Concretions of pyrite and marcasite are associated with bituminous coal deposits. **USE:** Heating fuel, industry, electricity production, and transportation. **APPEARANCE:** Black, often banded with layers of different plant material; will break into rectangular pieces. **ORIGIN:** Forms from the accumulation and compaction of peat.

## CHALK                    *Sedimentary*

**Group:** Sedimentary

**Classification:** Organic

**Grain Size:** Fine

**Mineral Composition:**
Pure limestone containing
calcite and small amounts
of calcareous mud

Chalk is a very pure form of limestone that was deposited by ancient seas that once covered western Europe. Chalk deposits are found along the southeastern coast of England and the northern coastlines of France, Germany, and Denmark. Nodules of flint and pyrite are commonly associated with chalk deposits. **USE:** Pigment for white paint. **APPEARANCE:** Powdery, porous, and very fine-grained; usually white or light gray, but can be red due to presence of iron. **ORIGIN:** Formed from the accumulation of microscopic sea organisms on the seafloor.

## SLATE
*Metamorphic*

**Group:** Metamorphic

**Classification:** Regional

**Texture:** Foliated

**Mineral Composition:** Primarily submicroscopic-size clay minerals, chlorite, quartz, and micas

Slate splits easily into thin flat sheets. It has been quarried for use as roofing and flooring tile for hundreds of years. Slates have a well-developed cleavage due to the parallel alignment of chlorite and mica flakes. The most famous sources are in Wales, with other excellent sites in Pennsylvania, New York, Vermont, Brazil, France, and Spain. Crystals of pyrite are one of the few visible associated minerals. **USE:** Roofing tiles, blackboards, pool tables, and flagstones. **APPEARANCE:** An extremely fine-grained rock that exhibits slaty cleavage; usually dark gray to black in color, but can be green or red. **ORIGIN:** Forms when fine-grained rocks such as mudstones, shales, and volcanic ash undergo very low-grade regional metamorphism.

## MICA SCHIST
*Metamorphic*

**Group:** Metamorphic

**Classification:** Regional

**Texture:** Foliated

**Mineral Composition:** Biotite and muscovite common; quartz, feldspar, and garnet (usually almandine) also present

Mica schists are found in areas of regional metamorphism throughout the world. They are characterized by a distinct foliation, or schistosity, along which they may be easily broken. Outcrops of garnet mica schists *(photo)* are common in the Rockies, the Alps, and the Appalachians. Associated minerals include beryl, calcite, garnet, pyrite, and stilbite. **USE:** None. **APPEARANCE:** A prominent schistose foliation with mica minerals visible to the naked eye; silvery white to gray, depending on foliation; medium-grained, with grains of garnet that can be an inch (2.54 cm) or so in diameter. **ORIGIN:** Formed under medium-grade regional metamorphic conditions with medium to high pressure; parent (original) rock may be sedimentary (for example, shale), volcanic igneous (for example, basalt), or other metamorphic rock (for example, slate).

## GNEISS            *Metamorphic*

*Gneiss*

*Augen Gneiss*

**Group:** Metamorphic

**Classification:** Regional

**Texture:** Foliated

**Mineral Composition:**
Similar to granite, with quartz, potassium feldspar, plagioclase, hornblende, and micas

Gneisses, which consist of streaked or segregated layers of light and dark minerals, represent some of the world's oldest known rocks. They are found in the Precambrian shields, commonly in association with granites and migmatites. Some gneisses are named for a particular characteristic. For example, augen gneiss has large eyes of feldspars (*augen* is German for eyes). Minerals associated with gneisses include andalusite, cordierite, garnet, and beryl. **USE:** Rough stone and polished slabs. **APPEARANCE:** Medium- to coarse-grained with discontinuous layers of light granular minerals, usually quartz or feldspars, and dark, amphibole or mica minerals; augen gneisses have large white crystals of feldspar surrounded by dark bands. **ORIGIN:** Recrystallization of clay-rich sedimentary rocks, such as mudstones, sandstones, or granitelike igneous rocks, during regional metamorphism.

## AMPHIBOLITE            *Metamorphic*

**Group:** Metamorphic

**Classification:** Regional

**Texture:** Foliated

**Mineral Composition:**
Containing hornblende and plagioclase feldspars

Amphibolites are often linked to copper-nickel and copper-zinc ore deposits. Like gneisses, they are found in the great Precambrian shields of the world, as well as Precambrian basement rocks in France and Germany. Associated minerals include magnetite, titanite, and, to a lesser extent, garnet. **USE:** None. **APPEARANCE:** Dark green to black in color with a coarse-grained texture; foliation may be present due to alignment of hornblende crystals; is sometimes banded. **ORIGIN:** Medium to high grade, regional metamorphism of igneous rocks rich in ferromagnesian minerals, such as basalt.

## ECLOGITE

**Group:** Metamorphic

**Classification:** Regional

**Texture:** Foliated

**Mineral Composition:**
Primary minerals omphacite (sodium-rich pyroxene) and garnet

Eclogites are dense high-grade metamorphic rocks that occur as small bodies or blocks in continental-oceanic subduction zones. They are formed in the lowermost crust and upper mantle, where igneous and metamorphic processes merge. Eclogites occur in zones of compression (plate boundaries), especially in California, the western Alps, Japan, and the Caribbean. **USE:** None. **APPEARANCE:** Dark colored, fine- to medium-grained rock that may exhibit weak banding; often contains garnet inclusions, giving it a mottled texture. **ORIGIN:** Metamorphism of ferromagnesian-rich rocks such as basalt at high temperature and pressure deep within Earth's crust.

## GRANULITE

**Group:** Metamorphic

**Classification:** Regional

**Texture:** Foliated

**Mineral Composition:**
Silica-rich granulites contain quartz, feldspars, and garnet; silica-poor granulites characterized by plagioclase, pyroxenes, and hornblende

The name granulite is derived from the Latin *granulum*, referring to the granular texture of the rock. Granulites are sometimes thought of as a variety of gneiss, but they form under more intense conditions of metamorphism. They occur in the ancient Precambrian shields and in a few isolated areas in eastern Africa and India. Associated minerals include garnet, talc, tremolite, and anthophyllite. **USE:** Construction material and polished slabs. **APPEARANCE:** A massive coarse-grained rock with variable color depending on the mineral content; silica-rich varieties may be banded due to the presence of quartz. **ORIGIN:** Formed in the lowermost crust under the highest grades of metamorphism.

## MIGMATITE

*Metamorphic*

**Group:** Metamorphic

**Classification:** Regional

**Texture:** Foliated

**Mineral Composition:**
Quartz, feldspars, hornblende, and micas characteristic minerals

Migmatites are very high-grade metamorphic rocks that have been subjected to such high temperatures that they have been partially melted. This produces a mixed igneous-metamorphic rock consisting of granite intermixed with schists, gneisses, or amphibolites. Migmatites are generally associated with ancient continental shields, such as those found in Antarctica and Canada. Migmatites are not associated with any specific minerals. **USE:** Building stone; occasionally as polished slabs. **APPEARANCE:** Coarse-grained rock with a granular texture; often shows a swirled bandinglike appearance. **ORIGIN:** Regional high-grade metamorphism of parent (original) rock causes metamorphic rocks to be formed in some layers, while partial melting in other layers produces a granitic magma.

## HORNFELS

*Metamorphic*

**Group:** Metamorphic

**Classification:** Contact

**Texture:** Nonfoliated

**Mineral Composition:**
Micas, quartz, and cordierite major minerals in cordierite variety; garnet, hornblende, andalusite, and pyroxenes found in other types

This fine-grained nonfoliated rock is produced by contact metamorphism of shales. Found in California, France, Scotland, and Germany. A variety of minerals may be present, including andalusite, axinite, corundum, fluorite, and rhodonite. **USE:** Minor use as crushed stone. **APPEARANCE:** Dark gray to black in color; large crystals of cordierite give it a mottled look. **ORIGIN:** It forms where parent (original) rock, commonly a clay-rich sedimentary rock, is close to or touching a large igneous intrusion.

## QUARTZITE

*Metamorphic*

**Group:** Metamorphic

**Classification:** Contact or regional

**Texture:** Nonfoliated

**Mineral Composition:** Mostly quartz, with some micas and feldspars

Quartzite, consisting of more than 90 percent quartz, is a hard compact rock that has undergone such complete metamorphic recrystallization that its individual quartz grains are welded together.

When struck with a hammer, quartzites break right through the constituent grains, whereas sandstones break around the grains. Quartzite is found in many countries, among them Scotland, Brazil, India, Venezuela, as well as the U.S., especially in New York and the Carolinas. Associated minerals include almandine, epidote, kyanite, and wavellite. **USE:** Ceramics; glass manufacturing; foundation material for road and railway beds. **APPEARANCE:** Pure quartzite is white, but iron and other impurities can produce a pink or even deep red color; it has an interlocking texture of irregularly shaped grains. **ORIGIN:** Formed from quartz sandstone during contact or regional metamorphism.

## MARBLE

*Metamorphic*

**Group:** Metamorphic

**Classification:** Contact or regional

**Texture:** Nonfoliated

**Mineral Composition:** Composed essentially of calcite; pure marble white, but many color variations possible due to mineral impurities—copper, olivine, or serpentine responsible for green coloration

Marble is perhaps the world's best known metamorphic rock. Localities include Myanamar, Italy, Greece, Portugal, and, in the U.S., in Maryland, Colorado, and Vermont. Associated minerals include phlogopite, brucite, rubies, sapphires, copper, iron, tungsten, and zinc. **USE:** Most commonly used raw material for sculpture; important building materials, including both rough stone and polished slabs. **APPEARANCE:** A nonfoliated crystalline rock with interlocking and fused crystals. **ORIGIN:** Low- to high-grade contact or regional metamorphism of limestone or dolomite.

## SERPENTINITE                                        *Metamorphic*

**Group:** Metamorphic

**Classification:** Regional

**Texture:** Nonfoliated

**Mineral Composition:**
Varieties of serpentine
(for example, chrysotile
and antigorite) dominant
components

Serpentinite is the principal source of asbestos. The most famous serpentinite deposits are located in Quebec. Other significant localities are in South Africa, Russia, Cuba, and, in the U.S., in California and Montana. Serpentinite is associated with many metal and ore deposits, especially platinum, copper, nickel, magnesite, and iron. **USE:** Interior decorative stone. **APPEARANCE:** A fine-grained massive rock that has many slick, polished-looking surfaces caused by the shearing movement of the deforming rock. **ORIGIN:** Regional metamorphism of peridotite, pyroxenite (an ultrabasic igneous rock), and other igneous rocks in a water-rich environment; generally green in color, but can vary from yellow to dark brown.

## ANTHRACITE COAL                                     *Metamorphic*

**Group:** Metamorphic

**Classification:** Regional

**Texture:** Nonfoliated

**Mineral Composition:**
Carbon

The highest-quality, hardest, and cleanest-burning coal is anthracite. Although coal has a sedimentary organic origin, anthracite forms from the high temperature and pressure of metamorphism. Large anthracite deposits are found in China, Russia, Australia, and, in the U.S., in Virginia and Pennsylvania. Pyrite and marcasite nodules may occur with these deposits. **USE:** Iron and steel industry; synthetic-rubber manufacturing. **APPEARANCE:** A black homogeneous-textured rock, metallic in appearance; tends to break with a conchoidal fracture. **ORIGIN:** Intense high-grade regional metamorphism of bituminous coal.

## CHONDRITE                                           *Meteoric*

**Group:** Meteoric

**Classification:** Chondrite

**Grain Size:** Crystalline

**Mineral Composition:**
Similar composition to
peridotites and gabbros,
with pyroxene, olivine, and
plagioclase feldspar; small
amounts of nickel-iron also
present; matrix consists
of same minerals or glass

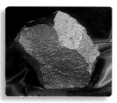

Chondrites form the largest group of meteorites classified within the stony meteorite category. Ordinary chondrites are very common and are found all over the world. One variety is the carbonaceous chondrite, which contains significant amounts of carbon, amino acids, and hyrocarbon materials. Scientists believe that this variety has the same chemical composition as the material that originally gave rise to the solar system. **USE:** Scientific research. **APPEARANCE:** Contains round silicate grains called chondrules; generally light gray to dark gray in color. **ORIGIN:** Uncertain; may be undifferentiated rejected material of planets.

# COLLECTOR'S RESOURCE GUIDE

*This handy reference guide includes
a chart of common mineral associations,
a selection of top mineral-collecting sites, and
a chart for identifying minerals by luster,
streak, hardness, and specific gravity.
A glossary of terms appears
on pages 182 to 185.*

# Minerals & Rock Types

The chart below lists some of the minerals that tend to occur in selected rocks. Their distribution and concentration is uneven since their formation depends on a variety of geological phenomena, such as volcanic eruptions.

## ROCKS AND ASSOCIATED MINERALS

| ROCK | ASSOCIATED MINERALS (OFTEN GRAINS, NOT DISCRETE PIECES) |
|------|------|
| *IGNEOUS* | |
| andesite | augite, biotite, horneblende, plagioclase feldspars |
| anorthosite | ilmenite, labradorite, magnetite |
| basalt | bytownite, native copper, quartz gemstones, zeolites |
| dacite | biotite, brown hornblende, plagioclase, quartz |
| diorite | copper, gold, ilmenite, titanite |
| granite (including pegmatites and porphyry) | antimony, beryl, bismuth, black tourmaline, cassiterite, copper, diamond, feldspar, garnet, gold, lead, mica, molybdenum, spodumene, tin, topaz, tourmaline, tungsten, zeolites, zircon |
| rhyolite | agate, cassiterite, chalcedony, copper, garnet, gold, iron, opal, silver, tin |
| trachyte | garnet, turquoise, opal |
| *SEDIMENTARY* | |
| chert | chalcopyrite, dolomite, galena, iron, lead ore, manganese, marcasite, quartz, sphalerite, zinc ore |
| conglomerate | native copper, gold, quartz, silver |
| limestone | agate, antimony, arsenic, barite, calcite, cobalt, copper, flint pebbles, fluorite, garnet, gold, lead, manganese, mercury, opal, sulfur, tin, witherite, zinc |
| sandstone | anhydrite, antimony, barite, calcite, celestite, chalcedony, gypsum, mercury, quartz, rock salt, silver, strontianite |
| shale | clay minerals, detrital quartz, feldspar, marcasite, mica, pyrite |
| *METAMORPHIC* | |
| gneiss | garnet, hornblende, mica, plagioclase, potassium feldspar, quartz |
| marble | brucite, corundum, diopside, epidote, gem serpentine, metallic ore, phlogopite mica, spinel, talc, tourmaline, vesuvianite |
| quartzite | calcite, copper, garnet, graphite, gold, iron, metallic ores, quartz crystals |
| schist | almandine garnet, andalusite, copper, corundum, gem serpentine, gold, pegmatites, talc, tin, vesuvianite, zoisite |
| serpentine | antigorite, chrysotile asbestos, garnet, gem serpentines, magnesite, mercury, nickel ores, pyrite, talc, tremolite |
| slate | andalusite, antimony, arsenic, coal, cordierite, gold, gold-bearing quartz veins, pyrite, quartz, quartz crystals |

# Twenty Top Hot Spots

Many rockhounds spend their weekends collecting minerals at sites within easy reach. Adventurous collectors, however, like to range farther afield. Fortunately, North America is full of sites—from the deserts of Arizona to the mountains of Quebec. On these pages is a list of twenty localities, selected from hundreds of excellent mineral-collecting spots across North America. The places were chosen for their variety of deposits as well as for their geographic scope. Some mines are famous for specific discoveries: Cave-in-Rock in Illinois, for example, is celebrated as the site where the mineral alstonite was first found on this continent. Other sites are esteemed as bounteous sources of a particularly prized type of mineral: Franklin/Sterling Hill in New Jersey, for instance, has a worldwide reputation for abundant fluorescent minerals.

**1 Green Monster Mine, Prince of Wales Island, Alaska**
This northernmost hot spot is the site of both epidote and quartz deposits.

**2 Butte, Montana**
Renowned for crystals of covellite, pyrite, and rhodochrosite. Also one of the most significant copper deposits known.

**3 Pala District, San Diego County, California**
Amazing crystals of a "shocking" pink tourmaline are common in this area. Kunzite, quartz, garnet, topaz, and cleavlandite also found here.

**4 Himalaya Mine, Mesa Grande, California**
Just north of San Diego, this mine produces red, green, and blue tourmaline; fine pink-orange beryl; topaz; and quartz.

**5 Virgin Valley, Nevada**
Best known for precious opals.

**6 Red Cloud Mine, Yuma, Arizona**
The best location for red crystals of wulfenite as well as smaller crystals of dioptase and cerussite.

**7 Mammoth Mine, Tiger, Arizona**
Famous for base-metal sulphides and vanadium. This mine also produces wulfenite, dioptase, and cerussite. Micromount-sized specimens found here are particularly beautiful.

**8** **Santa Eulalia, Chihuahua, Mexico**
A region known for its calcite, hemimorphite, silver, adamite, mimetite, rhodochrosite, and selenite.

**9** **Mapimi, Durango, Mexico**
This area has been one of Mexico's greatest locations for minerals. Finds include wulfenite, adamite, hemimorphite, calcite, and legrandite.

**10** **Crystal Peak and Pike's Peak area, Colorado**
Best known for its amazonite; also a site for goethite and topaz.

**11** **Tri-State District, Missouri, Kansas, Oklahoma**
Some of the finest galena crystals have been found here, along with calcite and sphalerite.

**12** **Viburnum Trend, Missouri**
This site is a rich source of the species of calcite, galena, and pyrite.

**13** **Thunder Bay, Ontario**
Beautiful samples of amethyst exist in this area.

**14** **Cave-in-Rock, Hardin County, Illinois**
Primarily a fluorite-producing mine, it is the site of the first recorded occurrence of alstonite in the United States. Witherite and calcite are also found in this area.

**15** **Keweenaw Peninsula, Michigan**
Home of the oldest metal mining in the western hemisphere; known for its pure native copper, silver, agate, zeolite, and datolite.

**16** **Mont St. Hilaire, Quebec**
Rich in serandite, catapleiite, and siderite, plus several very rare species—including ekanite, yellow wulfenite, and orange-red crystals of labuntsovite.

**17** **Mitchell County, North Carolina**
This district is home to fifty-seven different minerals, including emeralds, amethyst, rubies, sapphires, and garnets.

**18** **Franklin/Sterling Hill, New Jersey**
This world-renowned site abounds in franklinite, willemite, and zincite, among other minerals.

**19** **Jeffrey Mine, Asbestos, Quebec**
East of Montreal, this mine contains grossular garnets as well as vesuvianite.

**20** **North Shore, Bay of Fundy, Nova Scotia**
Around the Parrsboro area many mineral species are available, including zeolites such as stilbite, natrolite, gmelinite, analcime, chabazite, mesolite, and heulandite.

# Mineral Identification Chart

All the minerals included in the chart below are profiled in the Mineral Identification Guide on pages 96 to 153. The chart groups these minerals according to whether their luster *(page 80)* is metallic, submetallic, or nonmetallic.

Then, the chart organizes the minerals according to streak *(page 81)*, hardness *(page 81)*, and specific gravity *(page 84)*. Note that the streak for a great many of the nonmetallic minerals is either white or colorless.

| METALLIC MINERALS | | | |
|---|---|---|---|
| STREAK | HARDNESS | SPECIFIC GRAVITY | MINERAL |
| gold-yellow | 2.2 to 3.0 | 19.3 | **gold** |
| copper-red | 2.5 to 3.0 | 8.9 | **copper** |
| brownish red | 5.0 to 6.0 | 5.2 to 5.3 | **hematite** |
| n/a | n/a | 14.5 | **mercury** |
| silver-white | 2.0 to 2.5 | 9.7 to 9.8 | **bismuth** |
| silver-white | 2.5 to 3.0 | 10.0 to 11.0 | **silver** |
| light gray | 3.5 | 5.6 to 5.8 | **arsenic** |
| gray | 1.5 to 2.0 | 8.0 to 8.2 | **sylvanite** |
| gray | 3.0 to 3.5 | 6.6 to 6.7 | **antimony** |
| gray | 4.5 | 7.3 to 7.9 | **nickel-iron** |
| steel-gray | 4.0 to 4.5 | 14.0 to 19.0 | **platinum** |
| lead-gray | 2.5 | 7.4 to 7.6 | **galena** |
| greenish gray | 1.0 to 1.5 | 4.6 to 4.8 | **molybdenite** |
| lead-gray to black | 2.0 | 4.5 to 4.6 | **stibnite** |
| gray-black | 3.5 to 4.5 | 4.6 to 4.7 | **pyrrhotite** |
| gray-black | 5.5 to 6.0 | 5.7 to 6.9 | **skutterudite** |
| dark gray-black | 5.5 to 6.0 | 5.9 to 6.2 | **arsenopyrite** |
| greenish black | 3.5 to 4.0 | 4.1 to 4.3 | **chalcopyrite** |
| green- to brown-black | 6.0 to 6.5 | 4.9 to 5.2 | **pyrite** |
| brown-red to black | 5.0 to 6.0 | 4.5 to 5.0 | **ilmenite** |
| black | 1.0 to 2.0 | 2.1 to 2.3 | **graphite** |
| black | 3.0 | 4.4 | **enargite** |
| black | 5.5 to 6.5 | 5.2 | **magnetite** |

## SUBMETALLIC MINERALS

| STREAK | HARDNESS | SPECIFIC GRAVITY | MINERAL |
|---|---|---|---|
| red-brown to yellow or white | 3.5 to 4.0 | 3.9 to 4.1 | **sphalerite** |
| red-brown to black | 4.0 | 4.2 to 4.4 | **manganite** |
| brownish to black | 4.0 to 4.5 | 7.0 to 7.5 | **wolframite** |

## NONMETALLIC MINERALS

| STREAK | HARDNESS | SPECIFIC GRAVITY | MINERAL |
|---|---|---|---|
| white | 1.0 | 2.7 to 2.8 | **talc** |
| white | 1.0 to 3.0 | 2.0 to 2.5 | **bauxite** |
| white | 1.5 to 2.5 | 2.0 to 2.1 | **sulfur** |
| white | 2.0 | 2.3 | **gypsum** |
| white | 2.0 to 2.5 | 1.7 | **borax** |
| white | 2.5 | 2.1 to 2.2 | **halite** |
| white | 2.75 to 3.0 | 6.5 to 7.0 | **wulfenite** |
| white | 3.0 | 2.7 | **calcite** |
| white | 3.0 to 3.5 | 2.9 to 3.0 | **anhydrite** |
| white | 3.0 to 3.5 | 3.9 to 4.0 | **celestite** |
| white | 3.0 to 3.5 | 4.3 to 4.6 | **barite** |
| white | 3.0 to 3.5 | 6.4 to 6.6 | **cerussite** |
| white | 3.5 | 2.2 to 2.8 | **variscite** |
| white | 3.5 to 4.0 | 2.3 to 2.4 | **wavellite** |
| white | 3.5 to 4.0 | 2.8 to 2.9 | **dolomite** |
| white | 3.5 to 4.0 | 2.9 | **aragonite** |
| white | 3.5 to 4.0 | 3.7 | **strontianite** |
| white | 3.5 to 4.0 | 7.0 to 7.2 | **mimetite** |
| white | 3.5 to 4.5 | 3.0 to 3.2 | **magnesite** |
| white | 3.5 to 4.5 | 3.4 to 4.7 | **rhodochrosite** |
| white | 3.5 to 4.5 | 3.8 to 4.0 | **siderite** |
| white | 4.0 | 3.2 | **fluorite** |
| white | 4.0 to 4.5 | 2.4 | **colemanite** |
| white | 4.5 to 5.0 | 2.3 to 2.4 | **apophyllite** |
| white | 4.5 to 5.0 | 5.9 to 6.1 | **scheelite** |
| white | 5.0 | 3.1 to 3.3 | **apatite** |
| white | 5.0 to 5.5 | 3.4 to 3.5 | **titanite** |
| white | 5.0 to 6.0 | 3.0 to 3.3 | **tremolite** |
| white | 5.5 to 6.0 | 2.2 to 2.3 | **sodalite** |
| white | 5.5 to 6.0 | 2.5 to 2.7 | **scapolite** |

| STREAK | HARDNESS | SPECIFIC GRAVITY | MINERAL |
|---|---|---|---|
| white | 5.5 to 6.0 | 3.5 to 3.7 | **rhodonite** |
| white | 5.5 to 6.5 | 1.9 to 2.2 | **opal** |
| white | 6.0 | 2.6 to 2.8 | **albite** |
| white | 6.0 | 2.6 to 2.8 | **labradorite** |
| white | 6.0 to 6.5 | 2.5 to 2.6 | **microcline** |
| white | 6.0 to 7.5 | 3.5 to 4.3 | **garnet** |
| white | 6.5 to 7.0 | 3.3 to 4.4 | **olivine** |
| white | 6.0 to 6.5 | 2.5 to 2.6 | **orthoclase** |
| white | 6.5 to 7.0 | 3.2 to 3.5 | **diaspore** |
| white | 6.5 | 3.4 to 3.5 | **vesuvianite** |
| white | 6.5 to 7.0 | 2.6 | **chalcedony** |
| white | 7.0 | 2.7 | **quartz** |
| white | 7.0 to 7.5 | 3.6 | **staurolite** |
| white | 8.5 | 3.5 to 3.8 | **chrysoberyl** |
| white | 9.0 | 3.9 to 4.1 | **corundum** |
| white | 10.0 | 3.5 | **diamond** |
| white to yellow | 3.0 | 6.7 to 7.1 | **vanadinite** |
| white to gray | 6.0 to 7.0 | 6.8 to 7.1 | **cassiterite** |
| white or gray | 7.5 to 8.0 | 3.5 to 4.1 | **spinel** |
| white to green | 5.0 to 6.0 | 2.6 to 2.8 | **turquoise** |
| white or green | 3.5 | 4.3 to 4.4 | **adamite** |
| white or green | 5.0 to 6.0 | 3.2 to 3.4 | **augite** |
| white to gray or green | 5.0 to 6.0 | 3.3 to 3.5 | **diopside** |
| white to pale blue | 2.0 to 4.0 | 2.0 to 2.4 | **chrysocolla** |
| colorless | 2.5 to 3.0 | 2.8 to 2.9 | **muscovite** |
| colorless | 2.5 to 3.0 | 2.8 to 2.9 | **lepidolite** |
| colorless | 2.5 to 3.0 | 2.8 to 3.4 | **biotite** |
| colorless | 3.5 to 4.0 | 2.1 to 2.2 | **stilbite** |
| colorless | 4.0 to 7.0 | 3.6 to 3.7 | **kyanite** |
| colorless | 6.0 to 6.5 | 3.1 to 3.2 | **chondrodite** |
| colorless | 6.5 to 7.5 | 3.1 to 3.2 | **andalusite** |
| colorless | 6.5 to 7.5 | 4.0 to 4.7 | **zircon** |
| colorless | 7.0 to 7.5 | 2.6 to 2.7 | **cordierite** |
| colorless | 7.5 to 8.0 | 2.6 to 2.8 | **beryl** |

| STREAK | HARDNESS | SPECIFIC GRAVITY | MINERAL |
|---|---|---|---|
| colorless | 8.0 | 3.5 to 3.6 | **topaz** |
| colorless to gray | 5.5 to 6.0 | 3.2 to 3.9 | **enstatite** |
| colorless to gray | 6.0 to 7.0 | 3.4 to 3.5 | **epidote** |
| greenish or brownish gray | 5.0 to 6.0 | 3.3 to 3.5 | **hedenbergite** |
| gray-green to gray-brown | 5.0 to 6.0 | 3.0 to 3.4 | **hornblende** |
| bright blue | 5.0 to 5.5 | 2.4 to 2.5 | **lazurite** |
| light blue | 3.5 to 4.0 | 3.8 to 3.9 | **azurite** |
| pale green-blue | 5.0 | 3.3 to 3.4 | **dioptase** |
| pale green | 3.5 to 4.0 | 3.9 to 4.0 | **malachite** |
| bright to brownish red | 2.0 to 2.5 | 8.0 to 8.2 | **cinnabar** |
| brown-red | 3.5 to 4.0 | 5.8 to 6.1 | **cuprite** |
| orange-red | 1.0 to 1.5 | 3.5 | **realgar** |
| orange-yellow | 2.5 to 3.0 | 5.9 to 6.1 | **crocoite** |
| pale yellow | 1.0 to 1.5 | 3.4 to 3.5 | **orpiment** |
| yellow | 2.0 to 2.5 | 3.2 | **autunite** |
| yellow to brown | 5.0 to 5.5 | 3.3 to 4.3 | **goethite** |
| yellow to brown | up to 5.5 | 2.7 to 4.3 | **limonite** |
| reddish brown | 5.0 to 6.0 | 3.2 | **neptunite** |
| pale brown | 6.0 to 6.5 | 4.2 to 4.4 | **rutile** |

# Important Addresses

## URLS

**www.minsocam.org**
Mineralogical Society of America: Information on everything from workshops and shows to associations and books.

**www.usgs.gov/**
U.S. Geological Survey: Information on geological formations nationwide.

**www.rockhounds.com**
Bob's Rock Shop: Best site for hot links to other rock and mineral websites.

**http://pangea.usask.ca/~dfs846/rmac/**
The Canadian Directory of Rock and Mineral Associations: Hot links to all the major gem and mineral associations in Canada.

**www.minrec.org**
*The Mineralogical Record* magazine online.

**www.amnh.org**
American Museum of Natural History: Information on the museum's mineral collections.

## ASSOCIATIONS

The Mineralogical Association of America
1015 18th St. N.W.
Suite 601
Washington, D.C.
20036

The Mineralogical Association of Canada
Cityview 78087
Nepean, Ontario
K2G 5W2

# Glossary

**Accessory mineral:**
A minerals found in such small amounts that its presence is not essential to the nature of the rock.

**Acidic rock:** A type of igneous rock (for example, granite) that is abundant in silica (minimum 65 percent). See also *Basic rock*, *Intermediate rock*, *Ultrabasic rock*.

**Asthenosphere:** Zone of Earth's mantle that lies below the lithosphere.

**Atomic number:** The number of protons in the nucleus of one atom of an element.

**Atomic weight:** The relative mass of one atom of an element or isotope; the sum of the masses of the protons and neutrons in the atomic nucleus of an element.

**Basement rock:** The oldest rock in a given area, composed of metamorphic and igneous rock underlying all sedimentary rocks.

**Basic rock:** A type of igneous rock (for example, gabbro) that comprises from 45 to 55 percent total silica. See also *Acidic rock*, *Intermediate rock*, *Ultrabasic rock*.

**Batholith:** A large mass of solidified igneous rock exposed by erosion that has either intruded into the country rock or been derived from it through metamorphism.

**Bedding:** Layering of sedimentary rock; beds are divided by bedding planes. See also *Strata*.

**Cabochon:** Gem that has been cut and polished to a domed surface.

**Caldera:** Large basin-shaped depression typically created by a volcanic eruption or collapse.

**Cleavage:** The tendency of a mineral to break along preferred lines determined by its internal atomic structure; minerals usually cleave parallel to crystal faces. See also *Fracture*.

**Conchoidal fracture:** Shell-like fracture.

**Continental drift:** The horizontal movement of continents relative to one another.

**Convection:** A mechanism of heat transfer in a flowing material heated from the bottom, in which hot material from lower down rises because of its lesser density while the cooler surface material sinks; currents formed by this mechanism drive plate tectonics.

**Core:** The central part of Earth; thought to be made of nickel and iron, and to be solid in center and molten outside.

**Country rock:** Rock that surrounds a vein or pocket of minerals; rock into which igneous rock intrudes. See also *Intrusive rock*.

**Crust:** The outermost layer of the lithosphere.

**Crystal:** A homogenous mass with its atoms and molecules arranged in a regular lattice to form a repeating network.

**Crystal axis:** An imaginary straight line assumed to pass through the center of an ideal crystal. Most crystals have three axes.

**Crystal faces:** The smooth, flat surfaces that form the geometric shapes of crystals.

**Crystal form:** The characteristic geometric shape formed by a crystal based on its internal atomic structure; a mineral will appear in a multitude of forms, all of which can be grouped within six crystal systems.

**Crystal system:** A way to organize crystals by the relationships of their crystal axes. Any crystal can be fitted into one of six systems: isometric, tetragonal, hexagonal, orthorhombic, monoclinic, or triclinic.

**Dendritic:** A term meaning arborescent or branching; used to describe a mineral habit.

**Detrital:** A form of mineral occurrence in gravels; detrital deposits consist of hard or heavy minerals such as diamond or gold. See also *Placer deposit*.

**Dike:** A wall-like igneous intrusion that cuts across the bedding of the country rock.

**Drumlin:** An elongated ridge of glacial debris, usually shaped like half an egg.

**Electron:** A negatively charged atomic particle.

**Element:** The fundamental chemical substances of all matter.

**Esker:** A long, narrow ridge of sand and gravel that was the bed of a stream under a glacier before it melted.

**Evaporite:** A sedimentary rock (or sediment) composed of minerals precipitated by evaporating seawater.

**Exfoliation:** A weathering process that involves the peeling away of thin layers of rock.

**Extrusive rock:** Igneous rock that crystallized on or near Earth's surface; sometimes called volcanic rock.

**Fault:** A crack or fracture in Earth's surface. Movement along a fault can cause earthquakes or, during mountain-building, release underlying magma and permit it to rise to the surface.

**Felsic:** An igneous rock derived from feldspar and silica; used to describe light-colored silicate minerals such as quartz.

**Ferromagnesian minerals:** Minerals consisting largely of iron and magnesium.

**Fluorescence:** The ability of certain minerals to absorb radiation and emit it again as visible colored light. Collectors use portable ultraviolet lights to test whether a mineral is fluorescent. See also *Phosphorescence*.

**Fold:** The deformation of rock strata into the shape of folds.

**Foliated:** Laminated parallel orientation or segregation of different minerals in metamorphic rock.

**Formula:** The chemical composition of a mineral (or other substance) expressed in chemical symbols.

**Fossil:** Petrified imprint or remains of animal or plant life preserved in Earth's crust.

**Fracture:** Breaking a mineral in a way that is unrelated to its internal structure; the surface of a fractured mineral is usually rough or uneven. See also *Cleavage*.

**Geode:** A hollow rock nodule, often filled with crystals.

**Habit:** The characteristic appearance of a crystal, determined by the way it formed.

**Hardness:** The resistance of a mineral to scratching and abrasion.

**Hydrothermal vein:** Formed by the crystallization of minerals from primarily hot aqueous solutions of igneous origin.

**Igneous rock:** Rock crystallized from magma or lava at or near Earth's surface; one of the three main types of rock that make up Earth's crust. See also *Extrusive rock*, *Intrusive rock*.

**Inclusion:** A defect or foreign object, gas, or liquid included within a rock or mineral.

**Intermediate rock:** Igneous rock (for example, syenite) having a silica content of 54 to 65 percent. See also *Acidic rock*, *Basic rock*, *Ultrabasic rock*.

**Intrusion:** See *Intrusive rock*.

**Intrusive rock:** Igneous rock that forced its way in the molten state into country rock and crystallized there; sometimes called plutonic rock.

**Ion:** An atom that has lost or gained an electron and become electrically charged.

**Isotope:** One of several forms of an element, all having the same number of protons in the nucleus, but differing in the number of neutrons and thus in their atomic weight.

**Kimberlite pipe:** Volcanic pipe-shaped structure filled with kimberlite rock that might contain diamonds.

**Lithification:** The process by which sedimentary rock particles are formed into rock by being recrystallized under extreme pressure.

**Lithosphere:** Earth's uppermost layer.

**Luster:** The manner in which the surface of a mineral reflects light.

**Mantle:** Intermediate layer between Earth's crust and core.

**Magma:** Liquid or molten rock; called lava when it reaches Earth's surface.

**Metamorphic rock:** Rock (for example, schist or gneiss) that has developed from igneous or sedimentary rocks due to intense heat and/or pressure; one of the three main types of rock that make up Earth's crust.

**Mineral:** An inorganic crystalline constituent of rock with a predictable chemical composition.

**Mohs scale:** A relative scale of mineral hardness reading from 1 to 10.

**Moraine:** Rock debris transported and deposited through movement of a glacier.

**Neutron:** An electrically neutral particle in the atomic nucleus having the mass of one proton.

**Outcropping:** Exposure of rock above the ground.

**Oxidized zone:** Layers in ore deposits where weathering produces secondary minerals.

**Paleomagnetism:** Magnetism exhibited by rocks containing iron minerals.

**Phenocryst:** Large crystals set in the finer-grained matrix of an igneous rock.

**Phosphorescence:** The ability of a mineral to absorb radiation and emit it again after the radiation has ceased. Collectors use portable ultraviolet lights to test whether a mineral is phosphorescent. See also *Fluorescence*.

**Pillow lava:** Lava that has cooled underwater in the form of pillows.

**Placer deposit:** Concentrated deposit of heavy, robust minerals, usually in rivers or seas.

**Plug:** The solidified core of an extinct volcano.

**Plutonic rock:** See *Intrusive rock*.

**Precambrian:** The period of geological time from the formation of Earth until six hundred million years ago.

**Proton:** A positively charged particle in the atomic nucleus having the mass of one neutron.

**Pseudomorph:** A mineral with the outward form of another species of mineral that it has replaced.

**Pyroclasts:** Rock fragments expelled from erupting volcanos.

**Radiometric dating:** A variety of methods used to date absolute ages for rocks and minerals based on the ratio between parent and daughter isotopes.

**Rock:** Matter that is made up of one or more minerals.

**Secondary minerals:** Minerals formed by the alteration of preexisting minerals.

**Sedimentary rock:** Rocks deposited in layers from preexisting rocks; one of the three main types of rock that make up Earth's crust.

**Sill:** A sheetlike igneous intrusion that has solidified between two sedimentary strata; sills usually lie parallel to the bedding.

**Specific gravity:** The relative density of a material, measured as the ratio of its weight in air to the weight of an equal volume of water.

**Seismic waves:** Shock waves produced in rocks by earthquakes.

**Strata:** Sedimentary layers. See also *Bedding*.

**Stratigraphy:** The study of the layered rocks exposed in outcrops.

**Streak:** The fine deposit of mineral dust left on an abrasive surface when a mineral is scraped across it. A mineral can often be identified by the color of its streak.

**Subduction zone:** Area where the oceanic plates move into the mantle.

**Twin:** A mineral specimen comprised of two or more crystals intergrown in a systematic arrangement forming a predictable twinning angle.

**Unconformity:** A rock surface that separates two strata. It represents an interval of time during which deposition stopped, erosion removed some rock, and deposition resumed.

**Ultrabasic rock:** An igneous rock (for example, peridotite) having less than 45 percent silica. See also *Acidic rock*, *Basic rock*, *Intermediate rock*.

**Uplift:** Causing a portion of Earth's surface to rise above adjacent areas.

**Vein:** A sheetlike layer of mineral material (ore, lode) that cuts across older rock.

**Volcanic rock:** See *Extrusive rock*.

# Index

## ST. REMY MEDIA

*President:* Pierre Léveillé
*Vice-President, Finance:* Natalie Watanabe
*Managing Editor:* Carolyn Jackson
*Managing Art Director:* Diane Denoncourt
*Production Manager:* Michelle Turbide
*Director, Business Development:* Christopher Jackson
*Senior Editor:* Elizabeth Lewis
*Art Director:* Jean-Pierre Bourgeois
*Writers:* Steve Krolak, Rebecca Smollett,
    Joan Kaylor, George McCourt
*Designer:* Hélène Dion
*Illustrators:* Michel Giguère, Patrick Jougla,
    Anne-Marie Lemay, Jacques Perrault
*Photo Researcher:* Linda Castle
*Researcher:* Adam Van Sertima
*Indexer:* Linda Cardella Cournoyer
*Senior Editor, Production:* Brian Parsons
*Systems Director:* Edward Renaud
*Technical Support:* Jean Sirois
*Scanner Operators:* Martin Francoeur,
    Sara Grynspan

*The following persons also assisted in
the preparation of this book:*
Éric Archambault, Philippe Arnoldi, Dominique Gagné,
Angelika Gollnow, Emma Roberts, Odette Sévigny, and
Esme Terry

## ACKNOWLEDGMENTS

*The editors wish to thank the following:*
Jill Banfield, University of Wisconsin-Madison;
Peter Bird, Concordia University, Montreal;
George Constable, for his editorial contributions;
John Groggs, Department of Natural Resources &
    Energy, New Brunswick;
Andrew Hynes, McGill University;
James Levesque, Geological Survey of Canada;
Wallace H. MacLean, McGill University;
Terri Ottaway, Royal Ontario Museum;
Ken Phillips, Arizona Dept. of Minerals
    & Mineral Resources, Phoenix, Arizona;
Robert A. Ramik, Royal Ontario Museum;
Walter R. Roest, Geological Survey of Canada;
Steve Scott, University of Toronto;
Carol Sheppard, National Mining Association,
    Washington, D.C.;
Otto Van Breeman, Geological Survey of Canada;
William Verwoerdt; President, Montreal Gem
    and Mineral Club;
Wendell Wilson, *The Mineralogical Record*;
Aaron Woods, Ocean Drilling Project,
    College Station, Texas.